WANDERING OHIO

Wandering Ohio

A Buckeye Trail Thru-Hike

Chuck and Beth Hewett

**Advice
from a
Trail**

Walk into beauty
Stay on your path
Find inspiration around every turn
Tread lightly
Pack life with good memories
Every day has its ups and downs
Watch your step!

--Ilan Shamir

Cover Photo by Chuck and Beth Hewett
Photography: Chuck and Beth Hewett

"Advice from a Trail" used with permission, Ilan Shamir at www.yourtruenature.com, #67221

Buckeye Trail Overview Map reprinted with permission of the Buckeye Trail Association

Copyright © 2017 Chuck and Beth Hewett
All rights reserved. No part of this publication may be reproduced, stored in a retrieval system or transmitted, in any form, or by any means, electronic, mechanical, photocopying, recording, or otherwise, without the prior permission of the publisher.

ISBN: 1542878861
ISBN-13: 978-1542878869

The Buckeye Trail

(Reprinted with permission from the BTA)

Contents

FOREWORD — 1

ACKNOWLEDGMENTS — 3

INTRODUCTION — 5

THE BIG LOOP — 13

SMART PHONES AND ROLLING HILLS — 35

THE WILDERNESS LOOP — 61

LOST TRAIL — 89

OHIO'S GEM — 105

TICKS AND SOUTHERN OHIO — 117

SOUTHERN TERMINUS — 153

MIAMI & ERIE CANAL NORTHBOUND — 175

EASTWARD BOUND — 209

FAMILY AND HOME — 237

APPENDIX — 259

FOREWORD

In November of 1958, an article entitled "A Buckeye Trail: So Far It Is Just an Idea" was published by Merrill Gilfillan in the *Columbus Dispatch*. The article proposed that Ohio ought to have its own long-distance hiking trail in the image of the Appalachian Trail so that "youth may have an opportunity to find inspiring recreation."

Less than a year later, in 1959, the nonprofit Buckeye Trail Association was formed by a small group of inspired and inspiring individuals such as Ohio's own Emma "Grandma" Gatewood, the first female solo thru-hiker of the Appalachian Trail. That year, the first 20 miles of a Lake Erie-to-Ohio River trail were blazed through the Hocking Hills region.

Over the years, the Buckeye Trail and its community have steadily grown in pursuit of that original great idea, and the BT has expanded to become, arguably, the longest loop trail in the country. The Trail's growth has come primarily through the contributions of time and effort by inspired volunteers.

Chuck and Beth Hewett are now two of those people Gilfillan was talking about in 1958 when he proposed that Ohio's BT "should be as endless and as boundless as the energy and the imagination of those who would use it."

I was happy to meet Chuck and Beth at the annual Buckeye TrailFest in 2013. I could sense their enthusiasm for the Trail, their love of adventure, and their love for each other. It wasn't long before Chuck stepped forward to volunteer for the BTA at our next TrailFest in 2014. A panel of BT thru-hikers discussed the need for a databook for the Buckeye Trail, and it was Chuck and Beth who volunteered to develop the book.

And they didn't just want to work from the comfort of their home—they wanted to ground truth it on their own BT thru-hike.

Today, the BT continues to evolve, bearing similarities to the Appalachian Trail as a long-distance hiking experience, but also offering its own unique experience. As of 2016, there have been less than two dozen individuals who have completed a thru-hike of the BT; but millions of hikers each year are enjoying a smaller portion of the Trail, each realizing the vision of that original idea.

From quaint towns, to urban centers, to the lonesome wilderness experience, from the beautiful vistas on well-maintained trails to the struggles of poor trail conditions, Chuck and Beth powered through to complete Ohio's long-distance trail. Along the way, they've had their own adventure that they tell here. Knowing Chuck and Beth and their unassuming natures, it is interesting to see how their adventure and love for the BT has inspired them to share their story in a public way.

And why? What is it about our state trail that encourages such great contributions that in turn inspire others to take a closer look at what can be discovered on foot around the Buckeye State?

The pages that follow hold some of the answers, but a full understanding is only to be found out there in Chuck and Beth's footsteps, following the blue blazes on Ohio's Buckeye Trail.

Andrew Bashaw
Executive Director, Buckeye Trail Association

ACKNOWLEDGMENTS

Our walk taught us about Ohio history, geology, geography, and most of all, the people who live in this wonderful state. We could not have even dreamed of such an adventure through Ohio had it not been for the original dream of Merrill Gilfillan, who in 1958 conceived a long hiking trail. We wish to thank the many hundreds of volunteers who have made that dream a reality, and over the decades have expanded and maintained the hundreds of miles of trail.

During the hike, trail angels encouraged and assisted us with a simple smile, transportation, guidance, an offer of drinking water, or a place to spend the night. There are many fantastic people in Ohio.

Chuck's parents, Bill and Evelyn Hewett, instilled in him a sense of adventure, a desire to find what is over the next hill or around the next curve, a drive to keep learning, and an appreciation of nature. Beth's parents, Ruth and Dave Walker, spent much time with their five children at the family cottage on Leesville Lake, as well as week-long tent camping adventures in Ohio and neighboring states, allowing her to grow up feeling close to nature. This also nurtured her outgoing personality, and on the trail, strangers quickly became friends.

Our thanks to our brothers and sisters, parents, and friends who read our daily journal, offering encouragement and thoughts about what made them laugh; what helped them feel our plight or amazement; and what information we were missing in our descriptions.

Our most ardent appreciation goes to our editor, Elaine Starner, who patiently guided us and spent hours creating this book. Without her assistance the flow and rhythm of the hiking story we have to tell would not have come to fruition.

INTRODUCTION

Standing in the drizzling rain on a gravel country byway, we looked up the wooded side bank to a tree that was clearly marked with a blue blaze. Those rectangles of blue paint mark the route of the Buckeye Trail.

What was not so clear was the trail itself.

Bushes and grasses pressed into and over the outlines of the path—capturing the drizzle and waiting to shower what seemed like buckets of water upon us as we passed.

Going up a steep hill is not easy in good conditions; in rain, through wet brush and grass, the hike is a muddy and slippery affair. Our rain gear kept us somewhat dry, but there was no relief for our feet as they grew soggy and squished with every step. I made a point of striking branches and leaves with my hiking poles to knock off the collected drops of water.

As Beth and I initially considered circling the state of Ohio by hiking the entire 1,444-mile Buckeye Trail, we were concerned by the fact that about 50 percent of the trail is on roads. But as we fought our way up the muddy woodland footpath that day, we really longed for a stretch of road where we could stroll along side by side!

As our hike progressed south from our starting point at Lake Erie to the southeastern hills of Ohio, the roads we walked increasingly traversed more rural landscapes. Traffic lightened as roads narrowed and some turned to gravel and dirt. Trees often lined the sides. We began to welcome the road sections. There the path is generally drier, the route more direct, the footing more certain. Open areas provide views of the countryside. Hikers doing short day hikes may prefer off-road sections; but when you are surrounded by nature for weeks on end, the benefit of woodland paths is diminished—especially when the trail is so lightly traveled as to be barely visible.

Most off-road sections were not as rugged as this muddy hill, though; and as the trail becomes better traveled, our feelings toward these few trail sections will undoubtedly change.

As a consolation, that day, the trail took us past beautiful sandstone outcroppings. Every little valley and rock fall was alive with the steady supply of rainwater. Wild geraniums, trilliums, and other spring wildflowers had burst forth with the blessing of water. Rain can cause many emotions: terror during a violent storm, or comfort as we fall asleep to soothing pitter-patter on a roof or tent. On that day, it built character as we pressed forward and hoped for a chance to dry out.

Day after day, as we moved onward through various weather and trail conditions, we reminded ourselves of why we took up this Buckeye Trail adventure.

⊕ ⊕

The idea of the Buckeye Trail (BT) was conceived on October 2, 1958, when Merrill Gilfillan (writing under the pen name Perry Cole) wrote an article for the *Columbus Dispatch* newspaper proposing a trail from the waters of Lake Erie on the north to the Ohio River on the southern border of the state.

A 14-member committee was created from interested readers; they met in May 1959 to form the Buckeye Trail Association (BTA). Among those in attendance was Emma "Grandma" Gatewood, who lived in Gallia County and had thru-hiked the Appalachian Trail in 1955. She was 67 years old at the time of her hike and the first woman to complete an AT thru-hike.

The Buckeye Trail as initially envisioned ran south from Lake Erie, then west through southern Ohio to Cincinnati. By the time that original trail officially reached completion on October 10, 1970, plans were already being made to expand the BT to encompass western and northern Ohio. Those sections were finished in 1980, connecting the four corners of the state and closing the "big loop." The BT now

INTRODUCTION

stands as the longest continuous hiking trail within any one state and the longest loop trail in the world.

The Buckeye Trail Association's quarterly publication, *Trailblazer,* was first published in January 1968. It provides members with information about hikes, trail maintenance schedules, and interesting stories about places and events along the trail. The BTA also supplies the latest updates on trail conditions, volunteer efforts, and other activities on their website at www.buckeyetrail.org.

I first learned of the 1,444-mile Buckeye Trail from my parents. Back in the 1980s, they had volunteered as trail maintainers, clearing brush and building bridges along the Massillon section, before the trail was converted to the multi-purpose path that it is today. However, I never took the trail too seriously until 2013 when my wife, Beth, and I attended the annual Buckeye TrailFest, a wonderful four-day event with hikes, tours, and presentations about camp cooking, trail maintenance, dehydrating food, other people's hikes, and much more. The volunteer effort to maintain and improve the trail impressed us, and the enthusiasm was catching.

I had hiked the Appalachian Trail in 2011, and in 2013-15, Beth and I hiked the 220-mile John Muir Trail in California, the 500-mile Colorado Trail, the Pembrokeshire coastal trail in Wales, and the Pacific Crest Trail (PCT) through the state of Oregon. Our growing immersion in the hiking experience gradually led us to think more earnestly about the long-distance trail in our own home state.

We attended the Buckeye TrailFest again in 2014 and were part of a discussion about creating a databook for the BT. Knowing how useful a databook is for long-distance hikes, Beth and I volunteered to work on the project. Over the next 18 months, many hours were consumed with gleaning information from BT map descriptions, Google maps, overlays, and county maps and then reformulating it all into a trail databook. The project taught us a great deal about the entire Buckeye Trail and also impressed on us the thousands of hours of work that have gone into creating the current maps and the trail itself.

During our 2015 hike on the Pacific Crest Trail in Oregon, we began to discuss testing the accuracy of what we had assembled.

Ideally, the information should be verified before publication of the databook. Since the book is intended to assist long-distance hikers or thru-hikers, we decided to experience such an undertaking ourselves. As a bonus, the hike would be in our own state.

✢ ✢

That October, Beth and I were bicycling the rail-trail near our home on a clear, crisp autumn day.

"We should hike the 57-mile Akron Section of the Buckeye Trail," I proposed.

Her response was quick.

"How about starting tomorrow?"

I was surprised, but she was right. The weather was beautiful for mid-October.

That evening, Beth contacted her sister Susan and her brother, Michael, to inquire about their schedules and ability to assist us. We also contacted Jim Sprague, the Akron Section supervisor, and he readily agreed to assist with a car shuttle.

We packed and the next day were on our way to meet Susan in Painesville for a ride to Brecksville, the northern end of the Akron Section of the Buckeye Trail.

This section of the trail heads south to a point north of Massillon. Part of the trail threads through the beautiful Cuyahoga Valley National Park. This national park was created in response to a nationwide concern over the destruction of our forests. Legislation passed in 1974 enabled the National Park Service to purchase land and use it to create national parks. The legislation gave the federal government the right of eminent domain to acquire land from private owners, for the good of all, and the government began purchasing land and houses throughout the Cuyahoga River Valley area.

The air was crisp and the sky clear as we walked along the woodland trail. Dry leaves crunched beneath our feet or rustled as we dragged our feet through them. Orange, yellow, and red surrounded us on that autumn day.

INTRODUCTION

The trail twisted and turned through the beautiful hills and ravines, under the color of the dominantly hardwood trees of the Cuyahoga River Valley. It passed near the lovely Blue Hen Falls, whose waters cascade over one of the many rock formations we traversed.

In a sense, the Akron Section is not part of the "Big Loop" of the Buckeye Trail. It is something of a "shortcut" between Brecksville Reservation in the north (at the junction of the Bedford and Medina Sections) to Crystal Springs in the Massillon Section further south. The building of this section created what is known as the "Little Loop" in northeastern Ohio. A thru-hiker wishing to complete the longest circle around the state unassisted would have to either miss the Akron section or hike its 57 miles in both directions.

This section was close to our home, and it provided an opportunity for us to test ourselves. How many miles could we cover in a day if we were not climbing up and over mountain passes, as we had done in so much of our previous hiking?

After several miles on the trail, I began to hobble.

"I'm getting leg cramps!" I told Beth.

We were not on mountainous terrain in high-altitude thin air, and yet I was getting cramps!

Beth cruised on by, seemingly unaffected.

"Your time will come!" I shouted, as I hobbled after her.

Our first day ended in the small town of Peninsula, and we sought out the Winking Lizard restaurant. After dinner, we walked to our car and drove to Susan's home in nearby Cuyahoga Falls. In addition to assisting with the day's car shuttle, she graciously provided us lodging for the night.

Our second day began with another car shuttle, this time provided by Jim Sprague, BT section supervisor. We parked our car at the south end of the Akron Section, where we would finish a two-day hike that would be primarily on the flat towpath of the Ohio and Erie Canal.

From 1827 to 1913, the Ohio and Erie Canal operated between Cleveland, on Lake Erie, and Portsmouth, on the Ohio River. Still visible along the towpath are locks, that raised and lowered canal boats, and aqueducts that carried the canal over side streams and even over the Cuyahoga River. At one point, beavers have dammed up the old canal, creating a large marsh, which is a favorite spot for bird watchers. Alert—and lucky—walkers might even spot a river otter.

Sleep does wonders for healing the body, and the next morning I felt much better. Beth, however, found that it was her time to pay some dues. Upon arriving at our motel destination in Akron that second night, she said emphatically, "I am not walking more than a couple of blocks to a restaurant!" A favorite Thai restaurant was 10 blocks away, but she was adamant. We found a small café and then settled in for the night.

On the third and last day of our trial BT hike, the trail exited Akron, the fifth-largest city in Ohio, on sidewalks and bikeways. The walk was pleasant enough through city neighborhoods and parks. At Summit Lake, a long, floating structure has been built to allow bicyclists and walkers to pass along the southeast side of the lake. Summit Lake is a large kettle lake formed at the end of the last glacial period, 10,000 years ago. The lake is so named because it is the highest point along the Ohio and Erie Canal, even though canal builders lowered the lake's level nine feet when they incorporated it into the canal system.

We hiked through Barberton, Clinton, and Canal Fulton before completing our Akron Section hike.

Our daily distances were approximately 16, 18, and 20 miles— distances we had done on previous hikes through mountains. Each day we had started two hours earlier: first at 11:30 a.m., then 9:30, and finally 7:30. Normally, our start time would be even earlier, allowing us to take more breaks throughout the day. While we did not have a definite projection of how many miles we could hike on a Buckeye Trail thru-hike, we did learn that any ambitious idea of 30-mile days at the start was not feasible for our aging bodies. Even relatively flat terrain can lead to muscle cramps. We speculated that in mountainous terrain our legs alternately use different muscles, whereas on flatter terrain the same muscles get overused and lead to cramping. It would take a few days to become acclimated to hiking every day.

INTRODUCTION

What were our expectations of a BT thru-hike? Granted, the Buckeye Trail would not have the breathtaking mountain vistas of the West, and sections of the BT are along roadways. No, this hike had to be thought of as similar to the Pembrokeshire trail in Wales, where we hiked along a spectacular coast, learned some history, and spent each night in a B&B inn. The caveat was that the Buckeye Trail is much longer than the Wales trail, it would not always provide glorious views, and overnight stays in B&Bs must be combined with tent camping and motels.

So let us now invite you along on a wandering hike around Ohio. On our own Buckeye Trail, we'll stroll through gently rolling farm country; climb the steeper hills of Southeast Ohio; admire massive sandstone and limestone formations; learn about Indian mounds, effigies, and ceremonial grounds; pause to reflect on dilapidated canal locks and aqueducts; and pay the fare to enjoy a serene mode of transportation of a bygone era. We'll come finally to the flat, expansive farms of northwest Ohio and walk along the Miami and Erie Canal and the rail-trails of the north.

We'll camp in a tent or enjoy bed and breakfasts and motels. Restaurants, diners, and cafés will introduce us to communities. Along the way, we'll meet interesting people and "trail angels" and learn about the Wright brothers, the Goodyear blimps, and the crash of a dirigible. We'll stop to visit museums for bicycles, forts, presidents, and Native Americans.

For those who attempt to follow in our footsteps, the path will not always be glamorous or easy. There will be struggles and inclement weather, but such times will make the highlights even more glorious.

If you're coming along with us from the comfort of your reading chair, you won't have to be concerned about leg cramps, obscured trails, poison ivy, muddy trails, or streams of rainwater cascading down over you. But if you do decide to meet the BT yourself, we hope our journal here serves as an introduction to a trail that will give you lifelong memories.

Come with us for a wandering walk around Ohio.

Chapter 1

THE BIG LOOP

Day 1: April 22, Friday

Well, the moment has arrived. Nearly 1,400 miles of trail lie before us, and our adventure is about to begin. The Big Loop will take over two months for us to complete.

My sister Sue and her husband, Brad, pick us up at 7:15 a.m. and drive us up to Headlands Beach State Park on Lake Erie. We chose to start at the northern terminus of the Buckeye Trail for two reasons: one, it is near our home and family; and two, we felt the most unique feature about Ohio is that its northern border lies along the 13th-largest lake in the world.

Pulling into Headlands Beach State Park, Brad parks the car near a granite boulder that was placed here just a year earlier by the BTA and state park personnel. Embedded in the stone is the plaque that commemorates the October 10, 1970, completion of the first segment of the Buckeye Trail, from Mentor, on Lake Erie, to Cincinnati, on the Ohio River.

Photographs are taken of our smiling faces at the Northern Terminus Rock and also along the shore of Lake Erie. Our expressions show the thrilling anticipation of the adventure ahead, but hidden behind the smiles is some apprehension. This is a long journey; we have no certainty of safe haven from the weather, a shower to wash off the day's sweat, and a soft bed in which to rest after a tiring day.

The Beginning at Lake Erie

We have done our homework, though, and our prior hiking experiences minimize the trepidation. Breaking from the comfort of a daily routine has infused us with exhilaration, and we venture forth, out to explore the unknown.

The hike to Painesville is along city and industrial-type roads, but once we are a little way through the town, the trail joins up with the Greenway Corridor hike-bike trail and takes us through some pretty country. Sue and Brad join us on a 2.2-mile stretch as the bike path passes through a woods. It is a pleasure to hike with them because of their lighthearted nature and joyful approach to life.

When the BT leaves the hike-bike path for a road walk, we say our final goodbyes. Sue and Brad backtrack to their car as we continue on with our adventure.

All around us are signs of spring as the earth comes to life. People are out doing yard work, trees are starting to show a little green, and some of the bushes are already out in leaf. It is a warm, 70-degree day under an overcast sky, with only a slight breeze along the trail.

We are thankful and relieved when some busy road sections are completed, but the more rural roads such as Cascade Road are a delight. This road follows the beautiful Big Creek, with its cascading waterfalls and gorgeous cliffs rising from pools of water. Along this road, we pass an unusual home that consists of multiple rounded concrete structures joined together. This place has been nicknamed the "Flintstone house." We wonder what the inside of it looks like and think it would be fascinating to tour the home. (It's a private residence, though.)

By coincidence, while we're passing the Flintstone house, we meet Patti Cook and her husband, who are driving by. Patti is the section supervisor for the Burton Section, which we are currently hiking through. In our conversation, she informs us that she is passing her section supervisor responsibilities on to another person.

After noon, we enter Girdled Road Reservation (a metropark), which has been nicely landscaped around the parking and picnic areas. The trail wanders through a wooded section, allowing us to relish in the solitude and the quietness of woods with only the chirping of birds and the sound of a small creek flowing by. We stop alongside the ravine and enjoy a snack of an apple and drink. A bench stands at the point where the trail crosses the stream, but someone reading a book has already claimed the idyllic spot.

As the trail through the park descends into a valley, the atmosphere changes. Here rich, damp black soil supports plants suited for cool and moist conditions. Annual and perennial plants push up through the leaf litter; and hemlock trees, which prefer a northern climate, thrive in the cool valley. As we hike along, we hear a woodpecker and an owl in the distance. What is an owl doing out in the early afternoon?

Road Walk

At Chardon (population 5,184), we find a maple syrup festival in progress. In a parking lot, we ask one man if he would know of camping options in the area. In the course of our conversation, he asks, "Are you packin'?"

I think to myself, *Of course we are packing; our backpacks certainly are not daypacks.*

Beth is thinking, *What does it look like, Mister?*

I start to mentally run through our equipment—tent, sleeping bag, change of clothes. Through my musings, I again hear, "You know ... are you packin'?"

Beth and I try to carry on the conversation in spite of this man's obvious lack of recognition of the gear we carry. But after we hear the question yet a third time, the light bulb goes off in my head.

I wonder if I should tell him that yes, I am, and he had better watch out if he approaches our campsite at night. Or, "Yeah, 'cause we've seen a chipmunk that looked like he might want to take us out."

I do not own a gun; and I figure that even if I had one, I would not be able to reach it when needed. Besides, I am on really good terms with the chipmunk population and will let them deal with any untrustworthy intruder in our camp.

At one festival booth, we decide to try a hot maple syrup stir. The concessionaire serves us a couple of ounces of hot syrup in a small cup. We stir the hot maple syrup until it turns a creamy white consistency like soft butter, and it is then a delicious, rich candy.

A large tent shelters several tables for dining, so we sit down to eat some of the food we are carrying. Good timing—a half-hour rain shower passes through while we eat!

South of Chardon, around 6:45 p.m., we turn onto a multi-purpose trail. Bass Lake Taverne & Inn is unfortunately full. We have no knowledge of any designated campsites along the trail, and so we hike on. When we spot a relatively flat area in the woods, we stop and set up our tent.

First Tent Site

By 8 p.m., we're snug in our sleeping bags and listening to the tree frogs. The thermometer shows 55 degrees. Our first day has come to its end.

We find ourselves tucked away in the woods, a safe distance from the bike trail so that we will not attract undue attention. It is not the comfortable inn where we had expected to stay, but it feels like a more exciting and appropriate way to start this adventure.

Day 2: April 23, Saturday

The woodpecker alarm goes off at 6:30 a.m., but we hit the snooze button for another half hour. It is 45 degrees, and we're not in a hurry to leave the warmth of our sleeping bags. The birds are up, and we hear a phoebe calling, as well as a towhee.

The marsh surrounding the area where we camped is actually the headwaters of the Cuyahoga River. About two miles into our hike today, we cross over a stream that is the beginning of a more defined Cuyahoga River. The morning remains cool and overcast. Our hats and gloves are still on as we hike. The first 4.5 miles are on a paved bikeway; then we turn onto a service road in Geauga County Headwaters Park.

As we approach East Branch Reservoir, we meet three people out for a morning walk. They inform us that if we look toward a peninsula as we go around the next bend, we will see a large, active eagle's nest. Finding the nest in the distance, we can just make out the head of the eagle sitting on the nest. What a treat!

Crossing over State Route 608, we return to the bikeway, which now goes through a golf course on a crushed limestone surface. We're surprised to see signs along Dunkee Road that advertise building lots for sale and an auction. Apparently the golf course is defunct and will be subdivided.

In another 0.6 mile we have a more pleasant surprise—a beautiful covered bridge. Down the embankment, someone has mowed an area and placed a picnic table. This is too inviting to pass up. We rest awhile and enjoy the view of the covered bridge and the stream tumbling over rocks underneath.

The trail is pleasantly peaceful through the woods as we walk on a bikeway and a service road. We see cardinals, goldfinches, red-winged blackbirds, crows, and several other birds. A horse-drawn buggy passes us on the bikeway. Geauga County has a large Amish population, and this part of the trail passes the farms and homes of these self-sufficient people. The buggy is a surprise; it's not something we expect to see on these trails.

Footbridge in Lake Metroparks

The serenity of the woods comes to an abrupt end when we step onto a two-mile section of road that leads into the town of Burton (population 1,460).

Entering the town of Burton, we briefly explore the town square before heading to our night's destination at the Red Maple Inn.

The inn was built in 1998 by Gordon Safran, who had owned 42 optical stores. For years, he and his family had come to Burton to relax. Finally, at age 61, when he decided he wanted a change in life, he sold the stores, and built this 18-room inn, using Amish labor and Amish-made furnishings. Throughout the inn, we also find numerous books about Amish life.

A wine-and-cheese event is held from 5:00 to 6:30 p.m. This event also includes soda, Chex Mix, nuts, three hot hors d'oeuvres, and puff pastries with a choice of cheese or mushrooms in the center. It is a very relaxing hour, enhanced by the scenes framed by the dining room windows—views out over the rolling hills of Geauga County.

In our room, I watch a little news while Beth enjoys relaxation time in the spa tub, one of the many amenities at the Red Maple Inn. What can I say? Some campsites are less rustic than others!

Day 3: April 24, Sunday

Morning dawns bright and clear. We scurry downstairs and out to the back yard, which overlooks a sprawling valley, to photograph the beautiful sunrise at 6:30. A layer of fog fills the valley below.

The morning is chilly at 32 degrees, so we linger over a delicious breakfast at the inn while watching the sun burn off the fog. We pack up, check out, and say our thanks for a lovely stay. We're on the trail by 8:15 a.m.

The first couple of miles are off-road, along fields. The sun glistens on the dew-covered grass and quickly warms the morning air. By 9:15, it is 55 degrees.

On the road walk, we see an unusual number of cars with canoes or kayaks. The Grand River canoe race was yesterday and boaters may still be relishing the thrill of a ride down the river today. Beth and I have entered that race in the past. With its high rock cliffs and side stream waterfalls plunging down to the river, the Grand River is one of the most beautiful waterways in the state of Ohio.

One car with a canoe on top passes us, and the driver must be an outdoor enthusiast; he gives us a wild, full-arm wave and broad grin.

Our walking pace on flat bikeways and roads is about three miles per hour. The average drops considerably when we stop for 10 or 20 minutes. Even such a short break in walking represents perhaps an entire mile that could have been covered. So to complete many miles in a day, we reduce our stops by keeping snacks in various pockets of our packs or clothing and pulling them out while we're hiking.

Beth spots an eagle flying east over the road. The sun glints off its white head, creating a brilliant, spectacular picture.

At the beginning of any hike, the body must adjust to the rhythm of hiking mile after mile for hours and days on end. On our first day, our hip joints immediately felt the weight of our packs. Fortunately, the second day was short, and we knew we were heading into a beautiful overnight stay. After last night's hot shower and rest, we feel much better this morning. Hopefully, our bodies will quickly adjust to the weight of our packs and the daily routine of walking.

Since today is mostly a road walk, I wonder what interesting events could happen. One answer comes as we trudge up a hill. A man comes out into his yard as we pass.

"Are you hiking the Buckeye Trail?" he asks.

He tells us he has hiked the trail a little bit and warns us that most of the trail is on roads. We, of course, know this from our work in drafting the databook. We learn that he once lived in Salem, Ohio, and had spent many summers at nearby Guilford Lake—where our home is located! What are the odds of that? Our conversation is a pleasant respite from the uphill hike.

Our goal today is Camp Asbury, just south of Hiram.

A half-mile before we turn onto the footpath leading to the campground, we see a lady stripping paint from a door laid across two saw horses in front of her garage.

"May we use an outside spigot to fill our water bottles?" we ask. She gladly shows us the spigot, and while filling our water bottles, we chat with her about our hike.

Back in the woods, spring flowers greet us—trout lily, spring beauty, trillium, cutleaf toothwort, and violets, to name just a few that are blooming on this beautiful, blue-sky day. Large leaves of skunk cabbage are also pushing up through the moist soils of the lowlands.

As the trail winds around, we encounter two large trees that have fallen across the path. We easily walk around them, and then meet a lady with pruning shears and a small scythe doing trail maintenance. We let her know about the two trees that are down, and she promises to call in the chainsaw experts. We talk for few minutes and thank her for her work.

The BT goes through Camp Asbury. At the lake, we cross the dam and find a bench where we sit down to relax. It is 3:15 p.m.; we have completed our 16-mile hike today in 7 hours. It is Sunday, the camp office is closed, and we see no one else in the area. Not much to do but snack and enjoy the sunshine and our front-row seat at water's edge.

This lakeside spot is grassy and flat, a perfect place to set up camp and enjoy the water views for the rest of our stay here. We hear a woodpecker softly tapping in a tree and search for it. Perhaps 20 feet up, the woodpecker is building a nest. It sticks its head out, and we see a little red patch, so it may have been a hairy woodpecker. At 7 p.m., we set up the tent, and we're off to slumber land by 8:30.

Camp Asbury Tent Site

Day 4: April 25, Monday

Morning dawns clear and chilly again—but this morning, we are in a tent, and the thermometer reads 38 degrees at 5:45 a.m. On mornings like this, you learn how to dress quickly and rewrap yourself in the sleeping bag to stay warm.

Once everything is packed up, we hit the trail, setting our sights on a warm McDonald's breakfast in Mantua, four miles away.

As we follow the trail through the woods, leave Camp Asbury, and turn right onto a multi-purpose trail, we see a small waterfall which has carved a large rock ledge into a modern impressionistic stone sculpture.

We are also leaving the Burton Section of the BT and beginning the Mogadore Section.

The BT is divided into 26 sections. We completed the Akron Section last fall, and the Burton Section we've just completed is the first in our hike of the 25 sections that make up the "Big Loop."

We breathe in the cool morning air and delight in the beautiful sunrise in the east and a near-full moon setting in the west. As we hike trails and country roads, we are immersed in glorious spring and our spirits are lifted.

We arrive at McDonald's at 8 a.m. and enjoy a warm breakfast. I make some quick trail notes, but we do not dally long—storms are forecasted for the afternoon.

On the outskirts of Ravenna, we detour about three miles into town to stay at the Rocking Horse Inn, an 1875 home that has filled many purposes over the years (even as a convent for nuns).

The current owners, brother and sister, purchased the inn as a B&B in 1999 and are continuing to restore the building. Amenities here include a sitting room, plenty of drinks and snacks, a jetted tub, a hot tub, and a tanning bed. After settling in, we go out at 5 p.m. for dinner at Guido's, an excellent restaurant. Beth has a salad, and I have a small salad and lasagna.

Back at the B&B, we meet the other guests, Paul and Jessica from England. Back in the 1960s, Paul came to the United States on a Fulbright scholarship to study physical education physiology at

Michigan State, a rather new topic at that time. He later started two universities, one in Singapore and the other in Ireland, and lived in both places for eight years. Later he opened a school in Hong Kong, stayed for four years, and left one year before Hong Kong was turned over to China. After raising their four children, Paul's wife, Jessica, received her master's degree in education and then found a job as a principal at a school for traveling people such as Gypsies. She worked there for four years before moving on to another school. It was a very-long-distance relationship for them during those years. They are in the United States now, celebrating the 50th anniversary of their marriage and his receiving his doctorate degree.

Day 5: April 26, Tuesday

The forecasted storm never materialized yesterday, but last night a storm awoke me at 4:45 a.m. and lasted an hour. At breakfast, our host informs us that we may also have slept through an earlier storm. The forecast is for rain from 10 a.m. this morning until noon, but the radar appears to show that the front has passed and we should be dry today.

We hope the radar is the more reliable, and we begin our walk out of Ravenna.

Oh—we have decided to fund our trip with money found along the way. So far, we have found a quarter, a dime and two pennies!

The trail leaves the road to join a footpath along Mogadore Reservoir. Horses are allowed here, as they are on much of the Buckeye Trail. While I dearly love horses, sharing a footpath with them is not always pleasant. Their hooves can tear up a soft path, and on rainy days, every hoof print fills with water, leaving the trail a muddy mess. Walking alongside the trail to avoid these muddy sections is difficult and damages trailside vegetation.

Wild animals have, so far, been scarce. We have seen signs of beaver—tree cuts at the lake at Camp Asbury and today at Mogadore Reservoir—and we've seen deer tracks. The only live creatures we've seen besides farm animals, though, are birds, ducks, squirrels, geese, and a chipmunk. Beth has also seen two beautiful blue jays today.

THE BIG LOOP

The forest around Mogadore Reservoir was planted in pine trees long ago, and now hardwood trees are starting to take hold amongst the pines. If natural processes are allowed to continue, a hardwood forest will eventually dominate the area. Walking through the woods, we see spring beauties, violets, May apples, and unfurling fern fronds. Rotting logs sport a beautiful green moss cover. Looking toward the lake, we see that some ambitious beaver has tried to take down several 12- to 18-inch-diameter trees, though we find no sign of a lodge. A yellowish bird flies across our path, probably one of the many types of warblers. Mogadore backwater arms are not deep, open bodies of water; rather, they are shallow and home to lilies, cattails and other aquatic plants. The noxious invasive garlic mustard plant is blooming along the trail and looking quite healthy.

The trail, which had joined a wide dirt service road, suddenly turns right, off that nice road onto a footpath. Apparently this path has not been maintained for a number of years. We bushwhack our way through briars, wild roses, and fallen trees. Then we lose the trail and must battle our way back to the service road, where we now see a blue blaze! Where had the trail come back to the service road? Or is the trail no longer intended to go off the service road? In a short distance, the trail again leaves the service road, this time to the left. This trail is properly maintained, and we can hike at a normal pace without fighting thorns.

Just before Congress Lake Road, the path turns swampy and we hop along on rocks, logs, and bricks that somebody has dropped in. At the road, we cross to drier ground, and suddenly two pileated woodpeckers startle us as they burst up from the ground into the trees. The sighting is an unexpected treat.

Tonight is a special night. My sister Joanne picks us up at the Mogadore marina and takes us to her home. We are doubly treated to find that my 88-year old mother, Evelyn, has happened to stop by on her way home from the McKinley Museum in Canton. Joanne's husband, Denny, and Sue and Brad also join us for dinner. A home-cooked meal, opportunity to do laundry, and catching up with family all make for a pleasant evening.

Day 6: April 27, Wednesday

"Trail magic," a phrase coined by long-distance hikers, refers to unexpected acts of kindness that lift a hiker's spirits and inspire gratitude. Trail magic appearing at just the right moment gives many hikers that little extra push that helps them along their way. Trail magic may be a candy bar offered by a passing hiker, stashes of water or soda in a cold spring, a cooler of snacks placed along the trail, a ride into town for resupply, or a gesture as grand as grilling food for any hiker passing by. The work of Buckeye Trail volunteers who each year devote hundreds of hours to maintaining the trail may be considered the ultimate trail magic.

Thru-hiking the BT is still in its infancy, so our expectation is that any trail magic we encounter on this hike will come either from family or in ways we cannot anticipate. We have already appreciated the wonderful kindnesses of my sister Sue, who took us to the start of our hike, and my sister Joanne, who picked us up last night and gave us lodging. Today's trail magic also includes a delicious breakfast.

To accommodate her morning schedule, Joanne drops us off at the Mogadore marina at 8 a.m. and then heads off to her yoga class. We continue down the trail.

The morning temperature starts off in the mid-40s as we hike the final four miles along Mogadore Reservoir. The first bird we see is a heron, then we spot a group of perhaps 50 migrating ducks sitting out on the lake. We also sight woodpeckers, blue jays, cardinals, phoebes, and more of the yellow warblers.

A couple out for a morning walk pauses to inquire about our backpacks. They live on Mogadore Reservoir and have this lovely trail passing their backyard. Meeting fellow walkers and sharing information about the Buckeye Trail is a delight.

Along our road walks, we find beauty in landscaping scenes surrounding homes, where crabapples, redbuds and other flowering plants are in bloom. It's nice to see that people care enough about their homes to make the outside attractive. The early morning haze burns off, and we bask in the warm rays of the sun.

We pass around Wingfoot Lake, which is part of the park once owned by Goodyear and operated for the recreation of its employees. It is now a state park. Our trail road takes us past a huge hangar where the *Spirit of Goodyear,* one of the Goodyear blimps, is still housed.

In early afternoon, the trail leaves the road and joins a footpath. We're now in Quail Hollow Park, and the temperature has changed noticeably, from 77 degrees on the road section to 67 degrees in this wooded section. It's a pleasant change as we make our way through the park to the primitive campground. Along the way, we see three gray squirrels, a black squirrel, and a chipmunk.

Quail Hollow State Park was established as a park in 1975 to preserve wetlands, prairie, and woodlands, as well as historic structures within its boundaries. The manor house was constructed in 1838 as a farmhouse. From about 1914-29, the Stewarts, railroad magnates from Akron, used the house as a hunting camp. By 1929, they had rebuilt the complex in its present form as their retreat.

Quail Hollow Tent Site

In mid-afternoon, we arrive at the camping area—a large, mowed area with a fire pit surrounded by benches and a picnic table. We locate a spot for our tent that should provide some protection from any adverse weather and have a cold dinner of trail food.

A long-distance hiker's mantra is "Keep it light." Beth and I have found we do not need a stove, fuel, or the associated utensils. We also do not build fires. In between restaurant meals, cold dinners (which are usually a flour tortilla wrapped around cheese and/or peanut butter) are acceptable. There are also instances when we may have a hot lunch and then we'll eat our backpack "lunch" foods for dinner. We have also ordered takeout from a restaurant and carried this special dinner until we reach a campsite.

Our backpacking tent is made of the very lightweight Cuben Fiber, and our hiking poles serve as tent poles. By reducing weight and bulk, we're able to use smaller, lighter backpacks, though we make sure our packs have comfortable shoulder and hip straps. (The appendix includes a complete list of our equipment and clothes.)

After every hike, hindsight has told us that we carried some items that were not necessary. That is partly because we don't want to sacrifice safety just for the sake of hiking "ultralight." We carry some first aid items and a few extra pieces of clothing in the event of extended inclement weather—though we hope we never have to use these items. On this hike, I also carry equipment for water purification.

Day 7: April 28, Thursday

This morning we are awakened at 5:30 by the soft pitter-patter of rain and, more pleasantly, by the calls of turkeys and phoebes. We check the weather radar, which indicates we may have two hours before the main rain event will be upon us. There's just enough time to hike to a restaurant and wait out the storm.

We pack up and are on the trail by 6:35 a.m., arriving at the closest restaurant, a McDonald's, at 7:20. Our hike into town is dry, but then, as forecasted, the rain begins in earnest at 8:30.

Beth sees three men sitting in a booth, says "Good morning," and they ask where we are hiking. She has a pleasant conversation with them about the Buckeye Trail, while I do some writing and looking ahead at our trail schedule. Since the trail goes through Quail Hollow, the men are familiar with it, but they are unaware of its full extent. They mention that Stark County Park Service is taking over maintenance of the park. This is considered a good thing; apparently, the county has more money than the state.

The rain continues for two hours. At 10:30, we walk over to Marc's grocery store for trail food—nuts, protein bars, and crackers.

Road Walk on a Drizzly Day

Then we are on the trail again, walking in a light drizzle. Occasional heavier downpours force us to use our Swing Trek umbrellas for the first time. These work like a charm. The umbrella handle slips between shoulder strap and body and holds the umbrella in place, leaving hands free. It is not windy, but we expect that even in a light breeze this setup should hold the umbrellas in place. The hands-free arrangement allows us to continue using our hiking poles.

The town we have just left, Hartville, marked the end of the Mogadore Section and the beginning of the Massillon Section.

We pass a home up on a hill, surrounded by a mega-lawn, and we wonder if the owner must have had dreams of medieval castles when he built his home up there. We also pass a mailbox constructed from an old fire hydrant and supported by pieces of pipe. Those are the most interesting sights for several hours.

We arrive at Pancho's restaurant at 2 p.m. and linger there for two hours, enjoying quesadillas while recharging our phones, writing trail notes, and checking the weather forecast.

✦ ✦

We are walking through a residential neighborhood when a kid comes running out of a house. He's all excited and wants to know if we are hikers and where we are going.

When we tell him we're hiking the Buckeye Trail, which goes around the state of Ohio, he asks if he can take our picture. We consent, and he runs back into the house to get his phone.

A picture by a power pole with a blue blaze would be appropriate. At least, that is our suggestion. The boy dutifully takes that picture, but he obviously has other images in mind. Could he take a selfie with us and post it on his Instagram?

And so, we become instant celebrities in his world of friends.

The boy's name is Keith, and he's in the seventh grade. He tells us he has hiked on the Appalachian Trail and has gone fishing many times with his father and has caught the largest fish of several types from the lake they frequent. We enjoy Keith's enthusiasm and conversation, but we have to bid him goodbye and move on. Such encounters make road walks more enjoyable.

At 5:30 p.m., we arrive at the Nimisila campground. The campground is closed, but there is little we can do about this, so we find a site and set up our tent.

An hour later, a Summit Metropark ranger arrives and inquires what we are doing here.

Apparently, a lady walking her dog had seen us and made the call to the ranger, reporting that two homeless people were setting up camp and that it had really "creeped her out." I suppose, to an untrained eye, our lightweight, Cuben Fiber backpacking tent does look a little like a garbage-bag shelter. And we are traveling with little equipment and no car or other means of transportation. But really, does "creepy" apply?

We explain to the ranger that we are thru-hiking the BT and need a place to spend the night. He takes our IDs and returns to his truck to contact his supervisor. Permission is obtained with no problem.

The ranger is very pleasant, and we talk with him for a while about our experiences of these first few days, our pack weight, and our lightweight tent; and then he leaves us to return to our rest.

Nimisila Campground

Day 8: April 29, Friday
Last night, the air felt cold and damp as we hunkered down in our tent. A light shower passed through and added to the dampness. Beth found the cold more penetrating than I did, but she slept enough to hit the trail for another day.

Physically, we are both settling into the rhythm of a long hike. But our mental fortitude is challenged when situations are less than ideal and we contemplate the long miles remaining.

Funding of our Buckeye Trail hike is progressing. Yesterday we added another quarter. We now have $0.62. We homeless people have to make the most of every penny!

This morning, phoebes greet us with their *fee-bee* calls. We hike past an osprey platform but do not see the osprey, although Beth heard their calls yesterday. We have seen kingfishers, cardinals, geese, killdeer, a hawk, and blue jays.

The road this morning is the busiest we have walked thus far on our hike. The traffic noise detracts from our feeling and sense of nature.

Eventually, as we head south of Portage Road, the traffic lightens, our bodies begin to relax, and we can again hear the birds singing.

Later, the BT blue blazes direct us onto the multi-purpose Ohio and Erie Canal Towpath. Here we are finally free of road traffic and can walk side by side on the wide hike-bike path of crushed limestone.

At 10:30, we stop at Riffils Riverside Grille at Forty Corners, along the Ohio and Erie Canal towpath. The restaurant claims to have an excellent breakfast. The building is not large and has a rustic feel, with dark wooden floors and furniture. It's perfect for a break, and we have a delicious meal to revive our tired bodies.

As we leave the grille around noon, the owner advises us to go to the bridge over the Tuscarawas River and look down to see redhorse sucker fish spawning. We are told the annual event lasts only one week; and when we stop on the bridge, we are fortunate to see dozens of the fish.

Continuing down the trail, we pass through Massillon (population 32,149). This town was founded in December 1826 and named after Gene Baptiste Massillon, a French Catholic bishop. The location was chosen to take advantage of the Ohio and Erie Canal, which was being constructed at the time. In 1828, the waterway reached Massillon, and the entire length of the canal was completed in 1832.

After hiking 10.5 miles from Riffils Grille, we arrive in Navarre (population 1,940) at 3:40 in the afternoon. Navarre is nestled on the banks of the Tuscarawas River. A missionary, Reverend Christian Frederick Post, built a log cabin here in 1761. Originally, the community was divided into three separate villages: Bethlehem, Rochester, and Navarre. The eastern section, Bethlehem, was the oldest, laid out in 1806 by Jonathan Condy as a Swedenborgian religious settlement. Rochester, to the west, was established next, in 1833 by Nathan McGrew. A year later and between Bethlehem and Rochester, James Duncan founded the town of Navarre. A financial depression resulted in fierce competition between the three villages, and in hopes of putting an end to the financially destructive and bitter rivalry, the community decided in 1872 to incorporate all three villages under the name of *Navarre*.

Ohio and Erie Canal Towpath

The Ohio and Erie Canal operated in and through Navarre until the Great Flood of 1913 damaged the canal so heavily that it was beyond repair.

We slowly make our way along Canal Street, looking in shops and restaurants, until we settle on the Firehouse Grille and Pub. We eat and relax there until 6:45 and then hike the last 0.6 mile of our 19.2-mile day. We camp in Pittman Memorial Park, settling in for a night along the Tuscarawas River. The murmuring riffles are sure to soothe us to sleep. Again, a woodpecker sounds in the distance.

Eight o'clock is considered "hiker midnight," and we strive to make that deadline each night. Tonight, however, Steve Walker and his wife stop by for a visit. Steve is a member of the BTA and will be publishing the BT databook. Our conversation is about the book, the trail, and the weather.

We have been fortunate in our first eight days—we've had no strong winds or storms. Also, cool days like the last two are nicely suited for hiking. After we say goodbye to our visitors, though, we gladly dive into the warmth of our sleeping bags.

Chapter 2

SMART PHONES AND ROLLING HILLS

Day 9: April 30, Saturday
Beth did not have a good night and had very little sleep.

Our campsite was at the bend of the river and on low ground, a very humid spot. Beth's sleeping mat has no insulation, and it was soon penetrated by the cold moisture from the ground. Extremely tired from yesterday's long hike, Beth had very little energy left in her body to produce heat. She began trembling as her body tried to warm itself.

My head had hit the pillow and I was already snoring, having no inkling of her distress. Beth began to shake violently, but she did not want to awaken me, knowing that we both needed our rest; and so she talked to herself, trying to calm down, thinking the shaking could be exaggerated because she was so tired. She covered up with anything she could find, but had no relief. Finally, she pulled a plastic rain poncho over her body. It did not breathe and seemed to hold the heat around her. At last, she fell asleep.

This morning, to her dismay, her sleeping bag is soaked. The poncho held in not only the heat but also moisture from her body.

We pack up and at 6:40 a.m. leave Navarre on the canal corridor trail. The morning is still chilly, at 41 degrees, and we have slipped on our coats and hats. The birds seem to be more active this morning—perhaps they are trying to warm up, too.

As we walk along the towpath, the trees protect us from the light breeze that is blowing. All we hear are our footsteps gently crunching on the fine limestone path and the chirping of birds. Along the way, we spot four deer, three rabbits, and our second garter snake—our first one was a few days ago. Along the canal, a blue heron keeps a few paces ahead of us until the water ends and it flies up, passes over an open field, and goes back to its favorite fishing spot. We have noticed that the underbrush is nearly in full leaf and now obscures our view away from the towpath. Everything is looking much greener than it was when we began our hike nine days ago.

Country Scene

At 8:30, the towpath leads through a culvert under a railroad track, and by coincidence, a train is passing overhead. We take several pictures to document the event.

A half hour later, we arrive at the remains of an aqueduct that once took the canal over the Tuscarawas River. The aqueduct has not been completely restored, but a bridge has been constructed to span the same area, and the stone piers that supported the aqueduct are still visible in the river.

An aqueduct was a wooden trough built to carry canal water over a stream or river. It was very much like a bridge—except that it was a waterway instead of a road, and the traffic was canal boats and horse or mule teams. A wooden walkway along the side of the trough accommodated the teams and their drivers. Aqueducts were expensive to build; only 14 were constructed along the 308 miles of the Ohio and Erie Canal. The alternative, whenever possible, was less expensive stone or wooden culverts routing smaller streams under the canal.

Aqueduct (near Bolivar)

In 7.7 miles, we arrive in Bolivar (population 996) and by 9:40 are comfortably seated in the Canal Street Diner. The place is bustling with activity, and we had a brief wait for a seat. A tourist might overlook this quaint diner, but it's obviously a favorite among the locals. Between the two of us, we have eggs, toast, home fries, omelet, blueberry pancakes, tea, cocoa, and orange juice. We spend a couple of hours enjoying the feast, reading and writing emails (using our smart phones), and reviewing upcoming trail information.

Smart phones are a marvel. Over the past several years, they have quickly and thoroughly invaded our lives, and now it seems there's nothing the phones cannot do. As we hike the BT, we use our phones to stay in touch with family; and while I walk, I use mine to record thoughts and facts for our journal.

This morning, though, I find there is a downside to walking and recording—my journal from yesterday has mysteriously disappeared before I could send it in an email to family members. This is a distressing discovery; it is difficult to recall details of sights, sounds, and personal encounters. Nevertheless, we must try to reconstruct as much of it as we can.

We thought we had more time to spend in Bolivar; the original forecast called for rain around 7 this evening, but now we learn the rain will be here as early as 3:30 this afternoon. We make a quick stop at the library to charge our phones and camera batteries. The librarian is very interested in our hike and requests contact information so that we might give a presentation upon completion of our hike.

A little after noon, we hurry to the Fort Laurens museum and spend 45 minutes viewing the displays. A group of Boy Scouts is also there, and someone has arranged for Chief Pipes of the Delaware tribe to visit and talk with the boys. From the chief, we learn more about the time when this small fort existed. His tribe was from the area along the portage path between the Cuyahoga River and the Tuscarawas River (many miles north of here). Chief Pipes sided with the British, but his brother sided with the Americans.

The Delaware and other tribes were natural allies for the British in their efforts to control the colonies. The Indians feared the westward pressure of the American settlers and hoped that a British victory would ensure the safety of their lands. The British had no territorial ambitions and had, in fact, attempted to prohibit settlement west of the Allegheny Mountains in 1763. The conflict was not over independence and philosophical concepts of political liberty and human rights; it centered on land—who owned it, who controlled it, and who exploited it. It is probable that the native tribes would have traded with either side, but the settlers' efforts to possess land, to cut timber, and to plant crops were viewed as an invasion of the tribes' traditional collective rights to the land.

Bolivar was originally an Indian village. Shingas, a leader of the Delaware people, established a village on the banks of the Tuscarawas River in 1752. The settlement was known as Shingas Town.

"Chief Pipes" and Beth at Fort Laurens

More than two decades later, George Washington wanted to establish a chain of forts along The Great Trail that ran westward from Fort Pitt (now Pittsburgh) toward northwestern Ohio. Washington hoped the forts would neutralize the threat from native tribes and, at the same time, serve as western supply posts for an attack on British Detroit. American General Lachlan McIntosh and 1,200 men left Fort McIntosh (now Beaver, Pennsylvania) and reached the area of Shingas Town on November 18, 1778. Fort Laurens was constructed in three weeks as a four-sided palisade with bastions at the corners, a blockhouse, and interior cabins or huts. The fort was named after Henry Laurens, president of the Continental Congress at the time.

McIntosh returned east to Fort McIntosh, leaving Colonel John Gibson with 176 men and five women to face the Ohio winter. Supply lines were too distant, and food and provisions were scarce. In early 1779, British-led Indians besieged the fort until reinforcements arrived in March. Later in the same year, the fort was abandoned.

We regret that we cannot talk more with Chief Pipes (or, his representative), but we know the rain is on its way. As we depart the fort, we cross a grand pedestrian bridge that provides safe passage over Interstate 77.

Farther on, we pass the remains of Locks 7, 8, 9, and 10 of the Ohio and Erie Canal. After suffering extensive damage in the Great Flood of 1913, the Ohio and Erie Canal was largely forgotten until efforts to preserve it resulted in the Ohio and Erie Canal National Heritage Corridor, chartered by Congress in 1996. The corridor stretches about 100 miles between Cleveland and Zoar, and much of the old towpath is now part of the Buckeye Trail.

Along the trail, a rufous-sided towhee sings *drink-your-teeeea* while a woodpecker drums in the background. A little later, the golden feathers of several goldfinches flash in front of us as they flitter along the towpath trail.

At 2:30, a few sprinkles catch up with us, and we deploy our umbrellas until the rain lets up about 45 minutes later.

Arriving at the Boy Scout Camp Tuscazoar at 4:20, we see the Boy Scouts who were at Fort Laurens—and hundreds more. What a time to stop at Camp Tuscazoar! Over 600 Boy Scouts have assembled here. They're working on an archaeological merit badge, which involves visiting several sites in the area and doing an archeological dig.

We meet the camp supervisor, Dana, and request permission to set up our tent in an area that will not interfere with the scouts. A site behind the maintenance building looks good, and Dana agrees to let us camp there.

As we set up the tent, the rain begins in earnest and does not let up. The forecast is for it to continue over the next 18 hours. It's time to relax and prepare for hiker midnight.

Day 10, May 1, Sunday

A light rain did fall most of the night, but we are fortunate that it has stopped by the time we're ready to pack up. We get on the trail by 6:45 a.m.

It is Sunday morning, and approximately one mile into our hike, we turn onto Bissell Church Road, where we pass Bissell Church, a lovely, small country church. A sign states that it was built in 1842, rebuilt in 1896, and remodeled in 1949.

We hike 45 minutes before we choose to remove our rain jackets and pull out our umbrellas. In the 60-degree air, it's cooler to walk without the jackets and let the umbrellas keep the mist off of us.

From under the umbrellas, our view is of mist-shrouded hills and valleys. The mist freshens the new growth on trees, shrubs, and grasses to a vibrant green. An olive-green plant puts out a wonderfully gentle aroma into the fresh, clean air. But the theme for today is the many dogwoods. Their lovely white blossoms stand out against the springtime green.

Beth just found a nickel. We are up to $0.67, as the homeless couple marches on.

Today's hike will be mainly a road walk; however, these mostly-gravel country roads are little used, and we can stroll casually and enjoy the scenery. One home has picture-worthy red azalea bushes and another innovative mailbox. The box is mounted on a huge pipe wrench, perhaps four feet tall. A very clever construction.

By 9:30, the rain shower has ended. Two hours later, the clouds part briefly while we rest on a bench situated right along the trail. It is probably private, but we are elated to find a comfortable place off the damp ground for a short break.

Along a township road, we're surprised to see a boulder, the size of a small billboard, with the following words neatly stenciled onto it: "This road is part of the Buckeye Trail." We have left the Massillon Section and are now into the Bowerston Section.

By 1 p.m., our shadows are following us. No place along the trail offers an inviting opportunity for a break, and we eat our trail food of nuts, crackers, and protein bars while we hike. However, our real fuel today is the promise of my sister's homemade apple pie tonight!

Gravel and Dirt Roads

The last couple of miles of our 18.6-mile day are through woods. Spring beauties, bluets, and May apples greet us along the way. Country roads are pleasant and make for easy hiking, but a good path through woods can provide real serenity.

The blue blazes are easy to find here.

While the Appalachian Trail (AT) uses white blazes to mark the official trail and blue blazes to mark side trails, the planners of the Buckeye Trail decided to mark the BT with blue blazes. This blue color was chosen because it would be more visible in a forest of green and brown or against a snowy white background in the winter.

Our destination is the marina on Leesville Lake. This lake was formed by a dam across McGuire Creek, a tributary of Conotton Creek. The dam was completed in 1936 by the Muskingum Watershed Conservancy District (MWCD) in accordance with the Flood Control Act of 1939 passed by Congress. It is the first of five MWCD lakes that we will pass on our walk around Ohio. The other four lakes will be Tappan, Clendening, Piedmont, and Seneca.

Trail angels, Sue and Brad, meet us at the Leesville marina at 2:45 in the afternoon. Over the past few hours, the clouds have again been thickening; and we are in the marina, talking about the trail and checking the store for thru-hiker supplies (limited, because it is early in the season and the store is not yet fully stocked) when the downpour begins. It lightens briefly, and we dash to Sue and Brad's car. The rain continues as we drive 30 minutes to a cabin on farmland they own nearby.

Once we are snug in the cabin, a brief thunderstorm passes through. But we are in a dry shelter and have a warm shower to wash off the sweat and aroma of *five days* of hiking.

Ahhh ...

Our spirits are lifted.

We spread out our gear to dry and enjoy trail magic. Sue has brought asparagus with egg sauce over toast for dinner—and, of course, the apple pie.

Day 11: May 2, Monday

Last night, additional storms swept through around 11:30 p.m. and 1 a.m. Then at 3 a.m., the heavens roared with a torrential storm. Lightning flashed, thunder crashed, and rain came down in sheets.

We felt cozy through it all and were so grateful for the shelter of the cabin. Would our tent have stood up to such a lashing?

Dawn is calm and peaceful, with fog in the valley and little sign of the storm that lashed out last night. We eat breakfast, return to the marina, and are back on the trail at 7:50.

Leesville Lake Path

Sue and Brad hike with us for the first couple of miles through the woods, from the marina to Autumn Road. Our conversation is about the wildflowers we see along the trail, naming the ones that we know and sharing memories that are triggered by the plants and flowers.

Once again, we say goodbye to Sue and Brad. Soon after, we find a historic marker along the road. It reads:

> New Hagerstown Academy, built on this site in 1837, operated as a fully qualified educational institution until the turn of the century. It offered a well-rounded

curriculum and some of the most eminent physicians, lawyers, educators, and business administrators of those days received their training here. The last principal of the academy was Professor John Howard Brown.

It seems strange that an academy once flourished here in a part of Ohio that is now so rural.

Another 1.3 miles brings us into Bowerston. Immediately, we are stopped by a lady in front of her house who is very excited to see Buckeye Trail hikers. She tells us about growing up on an 80-acre farm near the plaque we had just seen about the academy. She tells us about her many life decisions: selling and buying property, painting houses, managing rentals, and operating an antique store. We could talk longer—*she* could talk longer—but the Western Grill restaurant is calling, and so we bid her and her four-year-old daughter goodbye.

Even though it is 11 a.m., the waitress lets us order from the breakfast menu. We also order two cheese sandwiches for the trail.

Four guys in the restaurant comment about our backpacks and really take an interest in our hike. They ask how far we've hiked, what the Buckeye Trail is, and where it goes around the state. In general, people know a little about the trail but are astonished to hear about its full extent.

A mile out of town, we enjoy our walk along Willis Creek Road. A creek runs along the left side and the woods beyond looks particularly enchanting in its spring foliage. To add to the magic, we see a couple of guinea hens; I haven't seen them for years. Then we come across a tree with eight large, pileated woodpecker holes. Besides the large size of the opening, the shape identifies them— pileated woodpeckers create an opening that is somewhat rectangular.

In the Tappan Lake area, we are surprised to find beaver dams. We recently watched a PBS show that explained how beavers' activities transform a landscape. When they build a dam on a stream, they deepen the resulting pond by excavating large amounts of mud from the pond bottom for their dam construction. These changes to the pond also benefit other wildlife. Their sturdy lodges are generally surrounded by pond water, with an underwater entrance. They store branches below water (and ice) as their winter food supply. About three miles farther on, we come across an even larger complex of dams. What a wonderful sight! We hope this is one place where beavers will be allowed to live in peace.

Beaver Dam

Our late start to the day and the leisurely stop in Bowerston means we have to keep moving to make it to camp at a reasonable hour. Our destination is the Tappan Lake campground.

I expected the distance on the spur trail to the campground to be 0.2 miles, but it turns out to be a full mile.

So it's nearly 6 p.m. when we finish our 17.3-mile day, and there's not much time for evening preparations before hiker midnight.

Day 12: May 3, Tuesday

Well, we had an interesting night at Tappan Lake Park.

Since we had hiked into the campground on the spur trail, we didn't know anything about the campground layout. We set up camp near a shower house and restroom. As night fell, we realized this was not the best location—the light in that facility did not shut off. To add to our uncomfortable situation, a ranger came by a little after 10 p.m., woke us up, and very sternly told us that we needed to register and pay a camping fee.

I filled out the form, handed it back with $20, and told him we would probably be gone by 6:30 in the morning.

We returned to our sleep, only to crawl out of our tent at 5:40 this morning to see the ranger waiting in his truck a short distance away. As soon as we are packed and ready to move out at 6:10, he revs his engine and leaves the campground.

Clearly, we are not to be trusted!

We imagine him heading to the local hangout to tell his buddies about these two people who claimed to have walked into his campground on some trail he's never heard of. They had arrived without a carbon-emitting vehicle pulling a large tin can with a porch bedecked with dangling Christmas lights. They had just ... *walked!* Walked into camp with packs on their backs!

Perhaps he has already heard about the homeless couple roaming about the state.

Understand, there is nothing wrong with campers and all the accessories, but it's not the way we're traveling—and that seemed to have him flustered. Hopefully, his friends will attempt to explain to him what a thru-hike is, what the Buckeye Trail is, and that it really is possible to move around the state without a large SUV.

Despite this encounter, the morning is quite beautiful. A lovely sunrise lights our way as we take the park entrance road out to the town of Deersville (population 79!), where we find plaques describing the historic town and also the Moravian Trail.

Deersville was established in 1815 and reached its peak in the years before the Civil War when it was a stop on the stagecoach route between Wheeling, West Virginia, and Wooster, Ohio. Alexander Auld, a songwriter, lived near the community in the nineteenth century. His most famous song is "The Hills of Ohio," which has been considered from time to time as a candidate for Ohio's state song. The first verse is as follows:

> The hills of Ohio, how sweetly they rise,
> In beauty of nature, to blend with the skies,
> With fair azure outline, and tall ancient trees,
> Ohio, my country, I love thee for these.

The road from Cadiz through Deersville to the Tuscarawas Valley was originally a path that linked Indian villages. Moravian missionaries used the path as early as the 1750s, and missionary David Zeisberger came to the Tuscarawas River area via this road when he established the village of Schoenbrunn near New Philadelphia, Ohio, on May 2, 1772. Today the road is known as the Moravian Trail.

After a few more hours of hiking, we find a beautiful roadside rest overlooking Piedmont Reservoir, another Muskingum Water Conservancy District impoundment. The rest stop includes plaques about Confederate Brigadier General John Hunt Morgan.

In June 1863, Morgan and 2,400 mounted troops set out on a 1,000-mile march into northern states, starting in Sparta, Tennessee, going through Kentucky and then southeastern Indiana before entering Ohio. Some accounts say the campaign was intended to distract Union troops from other major battle points.

The Confederate raiders destroyed bridges, stole horses, and plundered supplies. By July, Morgan and his raiders were at the Ohio border and slipped into the state just north of Cincinnati on July 13. They headed across southern Ohio, hoping to cross back into Confederate territory at Buffington Island, West Virginia. But at a major battle there, they were repelled and Morgan lost 400 more of his men. (The cavalry's numbers had already been reduced on the march through Ohio.)

The remainder of the troops then turned northeast. When they reached the area we are now hiking through, their long march was almost over. By this point, Morgan's men were using whatever farm horses and wagons they could find along their path, and they were having difficulty keeping ahead of their Union pursuers. At nearby Hannah's Mill, they skirmished with local militia. In an effort to slow the pursuers, Morgan's men burned the covered bridge over the Stillwater Creek at Collinsport, a town now under Piedmont Lake. The Union forces were so close behind that they could see the burning bridge in the distance.

Morgan's Raiders would eventually be defeated and forced to surrender at Salineville, less than 50 miles from Deersville, on July 26, 1863. Morgan later orchestrated the most celebrated prison break from the Ohio Penitentiary in history. He was killed one year later in Greeneville, Tennessee.

S.S.S. *Hanna* Mooring Pin

On the shore of Piedmont Lake, the Buckeye Trail passes by an unusual sight for the hills of Ohio—a large dockside iron mooring pin, about 3 feet tall and 18 inches in diameter. The mooring pin is the only remaining piece of the S.S.S. *Hanna.* The "S.S.S." stands for *Sea Scout Ship*. The dry-docked ship, 133 feet long and 33 feet wide, was built of wood on a concrete slab by Hanna Coal Company in 1946. It served as a Scout sea camp, where Boy Scouts learned the use of signaling devices such as fog horns, signaling lights, and weather flags flown from a mast. Use of the ship was discontinued in 1960.

Piedmont Lake Camp

In addition to interesting historical accounts today, we find natural wonders in this area. On the Piedmont footpath, the red brilliance of the fire pink wildflower is easy to spot, and two patches of Virginia bluebells line the trail. A special treat is finding several groups of the parasitic squaw root. It is usually associated with oak trees and dependent on the host tree for nourishment.

We see beaver dams on the streams flowing into Piedmont, but they seem to be in disrepair, suggesting that trapping is allowed here and has adversely affected the beaver population. It is ironic that the MWCD has spent millions of dollars to keep sediment from filling the reservoirs—and the best system for accomplishing that is being killed.

At the Piedmont campground, we finish an interesting day. Our tent site is next to a small stream, whose gurgling lullaby will surely put us to sleep.

Day 13: May 4, Wednesday

At 5:40 a.m., it is still twilight, and we use a flashlight inside the tent to begin packing.

After packing the tent and filling water bottles, we are on the Buckeye Trail at 6:30—about 10 minutes after official sunrise. Climbing out of the Piedmont Reservoir area onto State Route 800, we have a panoramic view east toward the reservoir and the sun beginning to peek above a veil of clouds low in the eastern horizon.

On a dirt and gravel road, we pass a lovely redbud tree in bloom and then descend to a covered bridge. Even though our hike today will be on country roads, the roads are narrow and the trees press close, creating the feel of a wide footpath through a forest.

The 47-degree air is cool on our skin. Wild geraniums now join the many wildflowers bursting into spring, and a towhee sings his daily reminder to drink our tea.

Our route is generally west, so our shadows lead the way, and in the midday heat, they seem to perspire more as we go up the hills.

We hike over dirt and gravel roads and see farm animals, our first groundhog, rolling farmland, and rustic and dilapidated farm outbuildings (that are nevertheless picturesque). We pass a beautiful, abandoned brick church, which begs to be purchased and restored. Another special building along the trail is an old homestead. The siding on the two-story house is now a weathered gray and the window glass is gone, but judging from the window frame details, it must have been a very pleasant home for someone at some time. A spring house, a few feet away, may still be functional.

Rustic Country Scene

Just before we enter the wildlife section of Salt Fork State Park, a gray-haired gentleman comes out of a barn and asks, "Are you hiking the Buckeye Trail?" He seems genuinely interested in our progress, and Beth asks if he is from this area. Indeed he is! His family and his wife's family both lived on properties now within the park's boundaries. His wife, the youngest of her siblings, was born and raised in the only farmhouse that remains in the state park. It is the famous Kennedy Stone House, located at the water's edge and accessible by either footpath or boat. The house has been restored and maintained as a tourist destination.

Our hike today has covered a tiring 20 miles. We have finished the Bowerston Section and have begun the Belle Valley Section.

Looking forward to a stay at the lodge in Salt Fork State Park, we wearily turn onto the dirt road that leads away from the BT toward the lodge. A hot shower and a dry, comfortable bed, though, are still six miles away, and we're hoping we can hitch a ride.

As we start down the road, a truck also turns in. Beth flags it down, explains what we're doing, and asks for a lift to the lodge.

The truck has a crew cab, and we're invited to hop in. Our trail angels are hunting turkey in the area with other buddies, and they happened to be driving by to check on their friends. Apparently, they have time to spare, and they carry on quite a conversation about where they are from (Sandusky), some land they own in the area, and the hunting they've done in this part of Ohio.

They drop us off right at the lodge entrance.

How grand it is to be sitting in a beautiful lodge restaurant, eating a delicious dinner, and watching yet another rainstorm pass by while we are safely inside a building.

Day 14: May 5, Thursday

A zero day!

During a thru-hike, a day in which hikers do not hike farther down the trail is considered a "zero day." A "nero day" (i.e. near zero day) is when hikers camp close to town, leaving only a few miles into town where they intend to resupply, relax, and perhaps spend the night.

Today is cool and overcast with rain, mostly around breakfast and midafternoon. A good day to be in a lodge!

We spend our zero day enjoying good restaurant food, doing laundry, relaxing, and planning our venture into the challenging 115-mile Wilderness Loop of the BT.

Salt Fork is a 19,000-acre state park. It is said that the name was derived from a salt well located near the southeastern corner of the park and once frequented by native tribes. Brady's General Store, on a site close to the current marina, served the few hundred inhabitants of the area from the 1800s until 1940. (The store no longer exists.)

At 5 p.m., we sit down in the lodge restaurant, enjoy a delicious salmon dinner, and watch a 45-minute downpour outside.

Salt Fork dining room trivia: "Over 500 million straws are used daily in the United States. That's enough disposable straws to fill over

46,400 large school buses per year." We decide to turn down the offer of a straw for the rest of our journey.

We again meet Confederate General Morgan, depicted on a mural in the dining room. Morgan made several incursions into the Salt Fork area, and one of the hiking trails in the park is even named after him.

Day 15: May 6, Friday

At 6 a.m., the outside already looks bright. We pack and make our way to the Salt Fork Lodge front desk.

As we check out, we follow up on our request for a ride back to the Buckeye Trail. The staff is very courteous; they make a phone call to the maintenance person, and within minutes he is greeting us. His name is Matthew, and he's enthusiastic about giving us a ride back to the trail. He is from the Barnesville area, spent four years in Los Angeles, California, and is very glad to be back in Ohio where there are green trees and four seasons—in particular, the Christmas season.

Road Out of Salt Fork Area

The zero day has refreshed us. Back on the trail, the air itself is clean and fresh from the rain. Dogwoods are plentiful along the road as we hike away from the state park. The sun sparkles on the dew-covered grasses in the fields, the birds chirp merrily—and will we ever drink enough tea for that one bird?

Initially, our road walk is on a pleasant dirt/gravel road, but eventually we turn onto Fairgrounds Road, which is paved. There is very little berm, though, and the cars come flying by, so we must use extra caution. On hills, I jog ahead to the crest, listening for the sound of approaching cars and trying to minimize the time we are in the blind spot of passing motorists as Beth makes her way up. We're uncomfortable on this stretch; the road feels extremely dangerous for a hiker. It does have one good attribute—a beautiful, tall, cylindrical tree that is the namesake of our trail, the buckeye tree.

Fairground Road eventually takes us to the Guernsey County fairgrounds. To our good fortune, the gates are open. A horse show is in progress in one of the buildings, and we sit on benches at the fairground entrance, facing the sun and basking in its warmth while we eat veggie burgers we purchased at the lodge restaurant before we departed. The burgers are large, so we will enjoy finishing them at our next stop in a few hours.

We pass a significant milestone when we cross a bridge over I-70. We are now south of the interstate that cuts through the center of Ohio, and we will not be north of it again for a few weeks. As we plod south, the highway noise gradually recedes; we crest a hill, and silence envelopes us.

And then we dig out our sunglasses! When was the last time we used these? At this time of year, it is a pleasure to have to don them.

A herd of cattle that we pass seems particularly gregarious. I muse that they are either trying to keep the many young ones in order or else they are stating their contentment with the verdant green grass and warm sunshine.

A red-tailed hawk pauses in a tree to look us over, decides we are too big a morsel, and flies off.

The yellowish-green coloration of the forest has been gradually expanding. The oaks and a few other latecomers are finally opening their buds into young leaves as spring continues to unfold around us.

A little after noon, we take a break near State Route 265. Beth brought a lightweight red poncho, perfect to sit on during our rest stops, since the ground has usually been damp.

We arrive at Seneca Lake Marina and find that the marina campground is not open for the season. However the Parkside camping area, a little farther down the lake, is open and the marina staff graciously contact that office and ask them to hold it open until we arrive at 4:45 to check in.

Once there, we find our site and set up our tent. Beth relaxes while I explore the campground.

Bridge Over I-77

SMART PHONES AND ROLLING HILLS

Day 16: May 7, Saturday

This morning we have a beautiful sunrise over water! We watch it unfold as we hike along the shoreline of Seneca Reservoir. The sky brightens to blue as the horizon blazes in reds and oranges. A distant line of clouds plays with the colors and delays the rising of the sun by five minutes. We continue to glance back at the rising sun as we make our way out of the park.

Exiting the park, we have a woodland walk through dew-covered weeds and grasses. The trail is difficult to follow, and we have to be alert for every blue blaze. We scare a couple of deer along the way.

The trail descends from a hilltop into a private campground, and we lose the blue blazes. I know from the map that the campground exit is west, and we successfully make our way out to find blue blazes along a road. Shortly into the road walk, Beth spots our first turkey, in a person's yard.

We pass a house with two big dogs, whose deep barks can be heard echoing up the valley. We have constantly encountered dogs along the trail, and although our presence always makes them bark, we have not had any problems. Generally dogs are fenced or chained, and those running loose are usually friendly. Only once did we have a more alarming encounter—a bulldog followed us persistently, barking loudly. He came at us with a demeanor that said he would take off one of our legs if given a chance. I walked backward for a while, keeping my eyes on him and staying between him and Beth.

We turn onto Pipa Road and look back east. On the horizon, a large mound rises from a hilltop in the tree-covered countryside. Is it perhaps an Indian mound? It's worthy of a photograph.

Our morning rest is next to two large oak trees on a lawn of mowed field plants and grasses. The sun is warm on our backs as we give our hips and shoulders a break from the load they bear. In the sun, our little thermometer reads 90 degrees; but the air, with a light breeze, feels comfortable.

The trail takes us onto Shenandoah Road, a dirt and gravel byway. Its name is derived from the tragic crash of the USS *Shenandoah*, America's first lighter-than-air rigid airship and the first to be inflated with non-inflammable helium. Construction of the airship was completed in 1923 at a cost of $2.9 million. It was 680 feet in length, 78 feet at its maximum diameter, and 93 feet 2 inches in height.

On September 2, 1925, *Shenandoah* departed Lakehurst, New Jersey, on its 57th flight, a promotional flight to the Midwest that would include flyovers of 40 cities and visits to state fairs. Early in the morning of September 3, an area of thunderstorms and turbulence over Ohio caught the airship in a violent updraft that is thought to have carried it beyond the pressure limits of its gas bags. The airship was torn apart in the turbulence and crashed in several pieces. Fourteen crewmen perished in the crash, but remarkably, 29 men survived.

After the crash, the Navy's military emphasis shifted to airplanes. Several sites mark the *Shenandoah* tragedy because some sections of the airship were still buoyed by helium and drifted to nearby areas before crashing to the ground. Here we find a granite stone and kiosk with pictures and written documentation. The name *Shenandoah* means *Daughter of the Stars* in the Algonquin Indian language.

A half hour later, we turn onto a footpath which leads four miles toward Wolf Run State Park, our destination for the night. This state park is located in Noble County, the last of the 88 counties formed within Ohio (1851). In 1963, Ohio began land acquisition for the Wolf Run Park and completed the dam for the 220-acre lake in 1966. The state park was officially dedicated in 1968 and received its name from the Wolf family, who were among the first settlers in the area.

About one mile into the four-mile trail, the blazes are supposed to take us through a Boy Scout camp. However, when we arrive at the camp road, blue blazes clearly show we are to go left—away from the camp entrance.

We follow the blue blazes down a dirt road for about one mile— and then they simply end. Up to this point, the blazes were very clear, so we continue on the road perhaps another mile. Soon we are suspecting that this trail was mischievously marked to intentionally lead hikers astray, and we are no longer on the BT.

Beth sits down to rest, and I walk ahead to see if there might be any more blazes. I'm about to turn around, convinced we have been led on a wild-goose chase and ready to tell Beth we'll have to backtrack, when here she comes—riding up to me on an ATV!

We are again blessed by a trail angel. David stopped when Beth flagged him down and asked for information on the trail. A cheerful, outgoing father of four, he has been helping a neighbor get his tractor unstuck, and now he offers to assist us.

I climb aboard with Beth, both of us sitting on the fenders, and David takes us first to his home, where we switch to a more comfortable SUV. Then our trail angel drives us to the grocery store in Belle Valley. The store carries a sufficient variety of trail food for us to supply our upcoming, week-long hike in the Wilderness Loop. David bides his time by going to the car wash.

David then drives us one mile farther to our planned destination for the day, the Wolf Run State Park campground. We are very appreciative of his help; we took so much time following the wrong blazes today and now every minute counts this afternoon as we resupply and prepare for our hike into the Wilderness Loop tomorrow.

Sorting Food at Wolf Run Campground

At the campground, we check in, set up our tent, sort the food into daily rations, and eat dinner—egg salad and turkey sandwiches from the store in Belle Valley. Rain chases us into the tent, but it is short-lived and the radar looks promising.

Describing the Wilderness Loop, the BT section map warns that "Few services will be found along the route." Yet, it also describes this section as having a "pleasantly undeveloped nature."

We are about to test the accuracy of that description.

Chapter 3

THE WILDERNESS LOOP

Day 17: May 8, Sunday

Last evening, Beth stated in an email to my sister Sue, "I took a shower at the campground that has to last 7 days."

Sue replied, "I cannot imagine forgoing a shower after a sweaty day, and to do it for 7 days—no way!"

The Road Fork and Whipple Sections of The Wilderness Loop will offer few, if any, opportunities for a luxury such as a shower; the best we can hope for is a sponge bath.

Our tent this morning is dry, not even dew covered—a first on this hike. We are up at 5:20 a.m. and begin today's 20-mile hike at 6:00. It will be a little more difficult because we're carrying five days' worth of food, but today's route is 100 percent road walk.

Our destination is a lean-to on private property. The lean-to was built for the use of Buckeye Trail hikers, but we know of only one other possibility for shelter along the Wilderness Loop. I have no idea where we will be camping on the other five nights. What type of campsites will we be able to find? Where will we replenish our water supply? These are questions to which we have no answer as we start hiking this morning.

Today is cool and fresh, similar to yesterday. As we pass Caldwell Lake, a couple of miles out of the town of Belle Valley, the geese make a fuss on the water below us. This is a lovely country lake, nestled in a valley and surrounded by woods, and it has a small island.

A day park is on the back end, but it's out of our view; perhaps we'll have an opportunity someday to explore the lake from a kayak.

The three-mile road trail passing Caldwell Lake undulates. The downhills never make up for the slow uphill climbs. Along the way, we pass a rocky, 20-foot cliff with a stream undercutting it, the first time we've seen such formations since our start near Lake Erie. The trail is only briefly on State Route 285, and that is where Beth finds a nickel to bolster our hiking fund to 72 cents.

Today is Mother's Day. We made calls to our mothers last Thursday, during our zero day at Salt Fork when we knew we had cell phone reception. Just as we expected, reception in this Road Fork Section is limited.

Mother Nature is celebrating Mother's Day by giving us her best—our first cloudless morning. Coincidently, we started our hike on Earth Day, April 22, which is a special day to remind us to appreciate and respect the majestic existence we enjoy here on Earth. Let us not take our Earth and its wonders for granted any more than we take our mothers for granted. Resources cannot be extracted without consequences, and we should cherish all the plants and animals, for they sustain the web of life which, in turn, ensures our own existence.

Our morning rest stop is in the quiet warmth of the sun, with only a wisp of a breeze and the chirping birds to keep us company.

Then the blue blazes lead us onto Holman Road, a gravel road with no houses, trees crowding close, and a brook babbling that we must follow. We pass an opening created by a gas pipeline, and two red-tailed hawks screech as they circle in the thermals. Farther on, the trail wends its way onto an open ridgetop road, and from there we look back to a lovely brick church perched on the ridge. It is noon, and the bell tower strikes the hour before playing hymns on its chimes. The breeze carries the lovely melodies to us until they fade away as we hike onward.

We find another place to stop and rest a while. This walk is nothing like our hikes in the western mountains, where we sat on rocks and took in grand scenery. Rather, this rest is on a lawn, looking out over the green, rolling hills and meadows of southern Ohio. The beauty found in Ohio is subtle but no less special. The sun is warm and we feel a light breeze. On days like today, there is no place better to be than gazing over a beautiful countryside; we are sitting in a green cathedral on this Sunday. Letting nature flow around us is a powerful feeling. We love our home on a lake, but on a trail, a person "feels" nature and is part of it. We are at her mercy, both good and not so pleasant. Today is very pleasant.

Country Scene

At 3:05, we arrive at the lean-to. It is early, but here we have a place to rest, whereas the road ahead offers no guaranteed shelter.

The three-sided lean-to is constructed from untreated pine logs, and insects are breaking down the shelter walls. The roof appears to be made from old insulated metal garage-door panels.

There is no cell phone signal here, so I make written notes, waiting until a ridgetop road will offer us electronic connection to the rest of the world. I've figured out the mystery of my disappearing dictations. When I turn the phone on, I check for a signal before recording; but if at some point the phone loses the signal, it eliminates the email into which I am dictating my thoughts. So the moral of the story (that I eventually learned after a few lost entries) is to not do any dictation when the signal is questionable or when there is any chance that I might walk into a "dead" zone.

Log Lean-to

For dinner, we eat Fritos and cheese wrapped in flour tortillas. A red-bellied woodpecker is also having dinner as he works on a couple of trees nearby. We are surrounded by the green forest growth of early spring, and as hiker midnight approaches, we watch the evening light play on the leaves and tree trunks as we lie snug in our sleeping bags.

Day 18: May 9, Monday

Every time I awoke last night, a whippoorwill was singing. Counting its call is like counting sheep to fall asleep again. The continuous song never ends.

Morning arrives gray, cool (45 degrees), and without the promise of sun. Beth wears a coat and gloves, and I don a coat and hat. My hands are just on the edge of cold.

Our morning road walk begins at 6:25, and scenes of the morning include what looks like an original log cabin, a boulder in the middle of the road that recent heavy rains have loosened from the hillside, and a large creek with its water rippling over a gravel bottom under overhanging trees.

A light and steady rain catches us, but with little wind, our umbrellas do a superb job of keeping us dry. A mist forms over and among the trees and valleys, and moisture on the leaves and grass enhances their green brilliance. As we hike by a mule and two horses, they watch us, run off a little ways, stop to stare, and again run off. With our backpacks and umbrellas, we must appear as two very strange humpbacked creatures under silver domes. One horse lifts its tail and deposits a statement about our appearance.

Road T297 is dirt/gravel and is so little used that weeds grow down the middle. We pass many weathered, gray buildings, some still in use and others appearing ready to collapse in the next big storm.

Our hike is only 12.8 miles to the Lamping Homestead camping area in the Wayne National Forest. It will be a primitive site, and we're concerned about our supply of drinking water. Even though rain and clouds are forecasted, some drinking water will be needed for tonight and the next several days.

At the last house before we reach the camping area, the owners, an older couple, allow us to use the outside spigot to fill our water bottles and our red, three-liter water bladder. They assure us the water is safe to drink, but warn us about the taste. If we choose, they add graciously, there is a store one mile up the road where we can buy water. Not wanting to pass up any opportunity for a water supply, we fill our containers. Can we make do with one liter of water per day for the next three days? Or will we find clean streams where we can use our water-filter pump?

The campground has respectable pit toilets, six walk-in campsites, eight picnic sites, a picnic shelter, and a two-acre pond. Though the rain has let up, we head for the picnic shelter, which guarantees us a dry place to relax. We set up the tent under the shelter and settle in.

Then we sample the water obtained from the house—and the strong sulfur taste is unbearable! So I make the trek up the road to the store to buy water and also hope to find breakfast buns, snack items, and sandwiches for dinner.

Beth slipped on a stream crossing earlier in the day. Some roads cross a stream by going *under* the water—in the depression of the stream, a concrete bed has been installed to give vehicles a firm base over which to cross through the water flowing over it. Hikers also must cross the stream by going through the water. Unfortunately, the concrete can be very slick, as Beth unfortunately discovered today.

While I am gone, Beth approaches a family at the campground and asks if she can use their fire to dry her pants, still wet from her fall. They are about to break camp, but they not only grant her wish but also chop firewood, stoke the fire, and stick around to roast hot dogs. They have a light conversation about their favorite campgrounds and share camp stories, and Beth tells them about the Buckeye Trail and explains why she fell in the stream.

A sign at the camping area provides some history about the Lamping family, who were the first to settle here in the 1800s. Just southeast of the two-acre pond is an Indian mound where the family tombstones are located. No one is sure where the family came from or where the descendants of those buried here went afterwards. The sign adds a reminder about the hard life of the pioneers in the 1800s. They had to build their own houses, clear land for farming, dig wells, grow their own food, and endure drought, crop failure, and illness—just a few of the problems that arose.

Hmmm ... maybe a thru-hike is not really so hard!

Country Road

Day 19: May 10, Tuesday

An owl hooted last night, and in the early morning hours, the light, steady rain resumed. A whippoorwill greets the morning with its continuous, repetitive song, and lying in the tent, I wonder out loud to Beth, "When does a whippoorwill take a breath?"

We are in no rush to venture out from our dry shelter and start the day, so I write in our journal. By 6:05, we begin to pack up and prepare for the persistent drizzle that awaits us, certainly not the weather conditions we hoped for on a hike through the BT's Wilderness Loop.

The first 1.7 miles take us over two old iron bridges. Below, the streams play over a sand and gravel bottom, making ripples and pools that would be inviting on a sunny day.

We are in the hills of southern Ohio, so unless we are on a ridgetop, our view beyond our umbrellas is only to the nearest mist-enshrouded hillside. We have improved on our method of securing the umbrella for hands-free use—we wrap the umbrella handle strap around the backpack chest strap and then wrap our raincoat hood around the shaft for a second point of stability.

As the day progresses, the sky brightens slightly. The forest remains damp, and opportunities to sit and relax are difficult to find; so today is a slow, steady walk. Occasionally, we have short road walks between the long stretches of footpaths, and the contrast of the lingering dampness of the forest to the quick drying of the roads is striking. We also wonder if, as the BT was laid out, somebody took a page from the Appalachian Trail building manual—AT lore often jokes that the trail was created to find and follow the most torturous route over difficult terrain.

In spite of the wet conditions, the trail offers us its own trail magic. We pass beautiful sandstone outcroppings. And we see four box turtles! I have seen these creatures only a couple of times in my life, so this is a real treat.

The last part of today's hike is our best. It starts with a hike down Irish Run in a valley that is appropriately lush in green. The Buckeye Trail then joins Archers Fork Loop Trail, which must be used more regularly since it is the first footpath in this section that looks worn from use. How many people will need to tread the BT before it looks like this? So far, many of the BT footpaths appear to be used more by deer than by people.

The topography along Archers Fork Loop Trail also looks promising for campsites. We pass a set of sandstone boulders that may frame a good campsite, but it is only 3 p.m. and we choose to press on.

That decision turns out to be fortuitous. We find a beautiful ridgetop campsite in an area that was reforested with pines decades ago. Deciduous leaves now mix with pine needles on the forest floor as the hardwoods gradually gain dominance in the pine forest.

This is a dry site (no drinking water or stream), so the extra work of carrying more water today is rewarded. The water should last us to a road section tomorrow, where we hope to find houses from which to obtain additional water. We have not yet had to filter water from a stream, but some of the smaller streams we've crossed today looked very clean, so filtering and treating the water could also provide an acceptable water source, if necessary.

At 6:15 p.m., we eat our cheese wrapped in a flour tortilla, and the clouds part long enough to allow shafts of sunlight to streak through the forest canopy and brighten our evening meal. Today we had a long, continuous hike, so we soon let the birds sing us to sleep.

Camp near Great Cave

Day 20: May 11, Wednesday

At 5:30 a.m., the birds tell us it is time to get up, but we resist for about 15 minutes. Last night we received a decent rain from 9 p.m. until 11 p.m. and heard thunder in the distance, so other places may have been hit with a more severe storm. As we begin our hike, I again knock raindrops off branches and bushes.

On Archers Fork Loop Trail, we are soon awe-struck by two gorgeous sandstone formations in quick succession: the Great Cave, which by my estimate is 200 feet wide by 70 feet tall, and a natural bridge, maybe 150 feet wide by 60 feet tall.

We see two more box turtles along the path. We also pass a good campsite about one half mile before our first wet stream crossing of this hike.

Archers Fork stream is too wide to jump, and there are not enough large rocks to hop across. Our feet are already soaked from walking through rain-covered grasses, so we plunge ahead with shoes on. On the other side of the stream, we wring out our socks and slosh forward on the trail.

After crossing Archers Fork Road and climbing about 0.3 mile, the trail passes across the top of a massive sandstone formation from which a small stream drops, creating a thin line of a waterfall. Even the recent rains have not been enough to generate more than a trickle.

Wooded Trail

Our path remains wet and muddy, but the sun begins to show itself. Many puddles along the trail have tadpoles in them! Where do they come from? We pass over another sandstone structure with another trickle of water. The sandstone is covered with a rich, moist, sun-dappled moss—like a miniature fairy glen.

THE WILDERNESS LOOP

Leaving Archers Fork Loop Trail behind, the path is again less traveled. Moss covers sections of the trail, and little bluet flowers are pushing up through the moss. It's so pretty that we don't want to walk through it.

By afternoon, the woods are drier and the shade is a welcome relief. The sun's heat is a problem we have not faced for a few days.

The valley floor to our left drops further and further away as the trail leads steadily up to sandstone outcroppings. Green plants grow up to the base of the cliffs, providing a lovely contrast to the barren sandstone. Eventually we reach the ridgetop, and after enjoying a short flat section, we descend into a valley more v-shaped and without sandstone outcrops. At the bottom, we crisscross a small, trickling stream a few times before again ascending steeply.

Occasionally, we see—and have to go through—poison ivy. I am allergic to poison ivy, and its ubiquitous presence in Ohio certainly was one of my concerns for this hike. A person is likely to encounter it on any hike in the eastern United States. However, while we have been very cautious, so far there has not been as much as I expected along the Buckeye Trail.

Nor have insects been a major source of annoyance. Gnats began to appear yesterday and swarmed around our heads, but it was not a continuous nuisance, so we did not find them too troublesome.

On the ridgetop, the trail crosses a road that provides a reference point with which we can determine our position and the hiking distance remaining in this loop.

We descend again where two rivulets join. I enjoy a trail that follows a stream, and here we are treated to a long downstream walk. The stream babbles along and occasionally undercuts the sandstone banks, adding character and beauty to its course. Does this water flow year-round? Where might there be space for a shelter or tent? This is work that still needs to be done to provide information for thru-hikers.

The stream reminds us that the drinking water we obtained from a house earlier today has been consumed and we're in need of water for tonight and tomorrow morning. At a road crossing, we see a young adult at a nearby house. We quickly walk over to ask if we may refill our water bottles. After a short consultation with his parents inside, he agrees to fill our bottles. Our best opportunities for water are dependent on the generosity of people who live along these roads that we cross or follow.

We make one final ascent to a ridgetop and are close to leaving the Wayne National Forest. We'll have to find a campsite here on the public land. Ideally, a site should be flat, out of sight of any road, with places to sit and a stream to wash or filter water. Eventually, we settle for a ridgetop dry site that's not quite level and call it home for tonight. There is nothing special about this location—it's in the woods and near the end of a long series of off-road sections, but we are comfortable in our tent.

A couple of chipmunks running about prompt us to make sure all our food is in the food bag, a safeguard against hungry little creatures chewing into our backpacks.

We are beginning to stink. The odor is not noticeable while we're hiking; but in the confines of the tent, we notice we are getting ripe.

As we drift off to sleep, the only sounds are of birds chirping, a light breeze rustling the leaves, and an occasional distant jet.

Day 21: May 12, Thursday

This morning at 4 a.m., we again heard distant thunder, but only a small splattering of rain fell. Our tent remained dry, both inside and out—rather rare these past few days.

We use a lightweight, single-wall tent, so body moisture generally condenses on the inside. The two-person tent is forty-five inches wide, seven and a half feet long, and about four feet tall at the peak. Made of Cuben Fiber, it weighs less than two pounds and uses our hiking poles as tent poles. Though the Cuben Fiber floor is waterproof, we also use a Tyvek® ground cloth (eight ounces) to protect against sharp objects. The Tyvek® is also useful when we camp inside shelters; it protects our air mattresses from splinters and punctures.

An appropriate title for the past few days could be *What goes down must go up—and generally steeply*. The Buckeye Trail does not always follow the contours of a hill, nor does it use switchbacks to ascend or descend a hill. However, today we leave the long footpaths in the Wilderness Loop and hike on roads, where we can make faster progress toward Stockport, a destination that marks the end of this loop and represents dry shelter, a bed, and a shower—still a couple of days away. The roads do have their own ups and downs, but this is still easier walking than the woodland paths.

Country Road Daisies

In addition, the roads take us past houses, which hold a promise of replenishing our supply of drinking water.

At midmorning, we pass a trailer with two little kids looking out the window. The door is open, so we walk up and a lady comes out and happily agrees to fill our water bottles. The lady is babysitting her brother's two sons, and she engages us in friendly conversation. We talk a little about the surrounding farm, raising children in this rural setting, and, of course, about our hike and the Buckeye Trail.

We soon turn onto Tittle Run Road. Tittle Run stream is next to the road, and as we hike up the road, we find that it crosses the gravel road four times—without any culverts. The flow is shallow enough for us to use small rocks as a bridge to hop across. Long ago, construction of the road exposed sandstone along the side, and the sandstone is now covered with moss, ferns, dried leaves, and other forest plants.

Gravel Road Walk

Farther down the road, a pickup truck stops. The round-faced, smiling driver, Doug, is full of enthusiasm, curiosity, and questions. He was raised not far from here, operates a sawmill about two miles away, has three kids, and enjoys living in this part of the state. While still a young man without much money, Doug heard of some land being sold at auction and decided to attend. Because the day of the auction was rainy and unpleasant, very few bidders showed up; and Doug successfully acquired the land. He worked hard and little by little increased his land holdings. His sawmill is large and provides a good living for him and his employees.

Doug asks more intuitive questions about hiking than anyone we have met thus far. He inquires about the trail, our equipment, the blue blazes, shoes, feet, sleeping, and how we are feeling physically. We try our best to explain our three weeks on the trail and show him an overview map of the entire BT. The map is of special interest to him; he and his wife have discussed the blue blazes they've seen and wondered where the trail led.

He is so enthused about our hike that he wants to do something for us. He offers us bottled water, which we refuse—we have just filled our bottles. He gives us his phone number, in case we need anything. Then off he goes.

Pleasant Ridge Road lives up to its name, and we enjoy a relatively flat walk under an overcast sky. A box turtle is laboring to cross the road. I pick up the turtle and move it across the road in the direction it was headed. Did I make its day or ruin it? A pity I cannot speak turtle.

A hawk screeches overhead, an almost daily event. We have also seen snakes occasionally. All have been the beneficial and harmless garter snakes.

Incredibly, the trail takes us right past Doug's sawmill and Doug just happens to be pulling out in one of his big timber trucks. This time we do ask for water, and he hops out of his truck and retrieves two bottles that we graciously accept and drink heartily.

In our short conversation, we mention that we'll be heading to Wrangler Bar and Grill in Whipple. With a twinkle in his eye, Doug tells us to ask for the owner, Brian, who buys mulch from Doug. We're also instructed to send a picture of ourselves with Brian to Doug's phone.

Later, we pause for a rest along Caywood Road, and a family asks how we are doing and whether we need anything. We again receive an offer of water. People have taken an interest in our hike when they see our backpacks in diners or when they meet us ambling along on quiet country roads.

Beth points out that on our other long trail hikes, we became immersed in a hiking culture where we routinely met and talked with other hikers on the trail and at shelters. In stark contrast, we have not seen any other hikers on the Buckeye Trail, and it appears that there are *not* many other hikers—people we meet along the way are not used to seeing backpackers, and instead of embracing us as hikers, they're more likely to look askance at us and the walk we've embarked upon. So our interactions on this hike are different; we're meeting people who live along the trail and we're spreading the word about the Buckeye Trail.

⊕ ⊕

A solo hike, especially through the area we have just traversed this past week, would be quite lonely. I feel very fortunate that Beth is willing to share this experience with me.

Our story began back in 2013.

I had been on Internet dating sites for a number of years, hoping to find someone who both shared many of my interests and—equally important!—wanted to date me.

Beth and her previous husband were both from northeast Ohio but had worked first in the Caribbean and then in Lithuania, when the country gained its freedom from Russia. After her husband's death, Beth "temporarily" returned to the U.S. to explore what she might do. In a chance encounter with the dating website, she saw my online profile and sent me a message.

At that time, I was traveling and I did not respond to her inquiry. Amazingly, she wrote a second time—just as I was returning home.

I replied to her message and wrote that I would like to meet her.

On April 4, 2013, we met at The Blue Door, a café and bakery not far from her sister's home in Cuyahoga Falls. Normally, such a meeting involves a conversation over a meal, but Beth wanted nothing to do with that. My profile had stated that I was comfortable in a "green cathedral," and a walk in the Cuyahoga Valley National Park was what she wanted to do. That, in itself, was pleasantly intriguing. I found she was easy to talk with and seemed very comfortable enjoying the outdoors. After that, we enjoyed several pleasant hiking and bicycling outings.

I had previously made reservations to attend the annual Buckeye TrailFest being held in northeast Ohio. It was only a few weeks away, and I intended to tent camp for the three nights of the event. People at 60 years of age do not normally camp, especially having just met. But when I asked Beth if she would like to attend, she readily agreed. I had to admit to myself that I had never felt so instantly comfortable with someone as I did with Beth, and I looked forward to the outing.

The event ran from Thursday to Sunday. Beth had previously bought plane tickets back to Lithuania for that same Saturday, but when Saturday arrived, she chose not to get on that plane!

At the time, I knew little about the Buckeye Trail organization, so we both were going to learn a lot about it—and about each other.

About a mile after turning onto Reeds Mill Road, I spot a stream 200 feet to our left. The stream flows over an 18-inch-high concrete drive, obviously little used, perhaps only there for a farmer to access his field. I use this opportunity to take a sponge bath and rinse out my socks and shirt. A big improvement! Beth does not mind walking behind me now!

She also has an added jingle to her steps; she has found a penny and a well-worn quarter, bringing our fund total to $0.98.

We pass Berg Church, built in 1872, a small, simple structure without steeple or stained glass windows. Only the sign over the door and the cemetery behind it tell passersby that this is a church building.

Farther on, we pass the home of a person who must have wanted to live in a castle—and built one, complete with a turret.

We arrive in the small crossroads town of Whipple and head to the Wrangler Bar and Grill, where we meet the owner, Brian. He heartily agrees to have his picture taken with us, and we dutifully send it off to Doug. Kathleen, our waitress, treats us well as we rehydrate, linger over morsels of food, and make notes in the journal and databook.

We want to camp near Whipple, and when Brian hears this, he offers us a spot on property he owns. The site is near the river and has been mowed. It's also near State Route 821, but the traffic is light, and we sleep soundly.

Day 22: May 13, Friday

Friday the 13th. We are lucky. It rained all night, from 9 p.m. to 5:30 a.m., but when we were ready to pack up—no rain!

At 6:40, it is a lovely morning, 56 degrees, overcast, and holding the promise of a perfect, dry-hiking day. We leave Whipple with full bellies, cold French toast for breakfast, and sandwiches for lunch, all prepared for us by Brian's crew at the Wrangler.

The trail this morning is on a gravel road that winds through farm fields and occasionally through a woodland, where the chirping birds are closer and create a peaceful feeling, even though the traffic noise from Interstate 77 has become audible. A rooster crows, and the sun peeks out from behind the clouds.

Where the woods are on our left, the roadside is lined with Virginia bluebells and white flowers that look similar to baby's breath. Duck Creek is on our right throughout the morning; sometimes its course is close, and at other times it wanders to the far side of the valley. Side streams from the woodlands run clear before mixing into the muddy water of Duck Creek. At one place, we see the water churned into little rapids over a gravel bar.

Dogs bark at us from small enclosures. They're social animals and should be with people and have an area to run, and I cannot help but feel sorry for these animals as we walk by.

The French toast may be cold, but my, how delicious! We munch while we walk and watch goldfinches flitter near our path.

At 9 a.m., we arrive where the road crosses Duck Creek. Instead of a bridge, a low concrete structure with small pipes through it has been built for cars to cross the stream. When the water flow exceeds the capacity of the pipes, the creek flows over the concrete structure. Well, today the creek is pouring over it! A sign warns *Closed When Water Over Fording.*

Fortunately, the Buckeye Trail has an alternate route for such occasions. The alternate is longer by 0.4 mile, but our decision is made without hesitation. Before taking the alternate route, we linger to enjoy a snack by the river roaring over the concrete structure.

The second half of the alternate route turns off the main road onto a dirt road with a clear stream tumbling next to it. A red-tailed hawk flies from its perch, screeching at us for disturbing its morning. We pause long enough to watch a box turtle finish its trek across the road.

Fording

At 11:40 a.m., we arrive at the Dairy Food Mart near the I-77 exit at Macksburg. The convenience store is 0.2 mile north of the trail, but it easily reels us in for a rest, food, and, of course, ice cream. We use the time to catch up on emails and make reservations at the Stockport Mill Inn for Sunday night. We saw the mill last year as we explored the trail for databook information, and we are very much looking forward to our stay there.

Passing under Interstate 77 is a definitive milestone; it marks our completion of the eastern segment of the Buckeye Trail. Our travels now will be more westerly, toward Cincinnati. We will not cross to the eastern side of I-77 again until we are near Cleveland and in the final days of our hike.

This afternoon, a mail carrier stops along the road to ask where we are hiking from and where to? We show her a map of the Buckeye Trail. She is from the area; one of her grandfathers was a blacksmith, and the other worked with oil wells in the early 1900s, a time when nitroglycerin was used in wells, and, sadly, he was killed when a well charge exploded prematurely. The lady has been a mail carrier for 30 years and is very happy with her job—while working, she can be outside, enjoying nature, watching the seasons come and go in the rolling hills, and seeing new calves and wild animals along the way.

We hike on, intent on reaching one of two possible destinations for tonight's campsite. As we plotted our day, we marked a covered bridge on the map. That is one possibility. If the bridge doesn't have an appropriate area to camp, we'll go on to a cemetery that should not be much farther.

Later, we arrive at the point where the bridge should be—according to our map—and find that the hoped-for bridge does not exist. So we go on, now looking for the second option, the cemetery.

Our hiking day gets longer and longer.

And the cemetery never appears.

Finally, around 6 in the evening and nearly 24 miles into our day, we crest a hill and see a lady mowing the lawn around her farmhouse. We approach her and request a spot to set up our tent for the night. She graciously agrees. A true trail angel!

She even mows an area that looks suitable to us. We set up our tent and eat supper while she finishes her job.

Our trail angel is Gwen. She works at Memorial Hospital in the Billing Department, but she also has cows, chickens, hogs, cats, and dogs, and bales her own hay. She grew up in Beverly, where her father worked on the coal beltline that fed coal to the Muskingum River power plant. She tells us that she saw this house years ago and said,

"That is going to be mine one day." Her chance came several years ago, and she was able to acquire the property.

Since we progressed farther than planned today, we'll arrive in Stockport a day early. We call the Stockport Mill and make a reservation to stay Saturday night as well as Sunday. That will be our reward for today's long hike.

A whippoorwill entertains us as we prepare for hiker midnight.

Day 23: May 14, Saturday

The whippoorwill is calling again this morning. And rain is on the way! It looks like our hike today will be wet, windy, and cold, but we are looking forward to a joyful ending this afternoon.

We're fortunate to be able to pack up before the rain arrives. I leave a note in the mailbox to thank Gwen for a place to stay and to let her know she is one of our trail angels. I leave contact information, too, in case she wants to know about the rest of our trip.

We're on the trail by 6:30 a.m., and by 7:00, rain moves in and lingers with us for the next two and a half hours. The temperature remains around 50 degrees. We're dressed in hiking slacks, tee shirts, rain jackets, and hats. Our umbrellas keep our upper torsos dry, but the rain is accompanied by a wind that blows the rain onto our pants. When the rain subsides, the wind increases; and we're reminded just how miserably cold it can be when we are also wet. On the plus side, the rain has filled every rivulet and creek, bringing alive a myriad of waterfalls and flowing cascades.

At 9 a.m., we turn onto Onion Run Road, and enter the Stockport Section of the Buckeye Trail. This is cause for celebration: the Wilderness Loop is behind us!

However, our celebration is short-lived. On Onion Run, we soon find more of the low concrete structures for stream crossings instead of bridges. Cars generally can drive over these structures even after the embedded pipes have been overwhelmed by the water and the stream flows over the concrete. But for a hiker, the situation looks quite different.

At the first such crossing where the water is flowing over the top of the concrete, we dutifully take off our shoes and socks and wade across. This approach is tedious and time consuming, and pulling on soaked socks in a drizzle is not an easy task.

Less than a mile farther, we come to the next concrete crossing. This time, we just take off our shoes and walk across in stocking feet. This approach keeps our shoes from being completely immersed, but our socks are soggy and squishy when we put our shoes back on. We decide it is probably worth the time to remove both shoes and socks.

Stream Crossing in the Rain

A few more tenths of a mile down the road, we face a third crossing. Fortunately, this structure has been designed to handle at least this much water, and all the water is flowing through the pipes. We cross over the concrete depression without further soaking of our shoes and socks. It is still 50 degrees, though, and the drizzle is still coming down.

THE WILDERNESS LOOP

Reaching Olney Run Road, we soon must make a decision. The road follows the stream known as Olney Run, and the map instructs us to take Groah Road south and then to "ford Olney Run."

But Olney Run is a swollen torrent.

Beth and I look at the swirling water and then at each other and agree: "No way are we fording Olney Run!"

The recommended point of fording is a mile or so upstream. Granted, the stream may be smaller at that point, but we are not interested in hiking up the road just to find that we would have to turn around at the stream crossing or risk being swept away in the torrent.

I study the map and find an alternate route. The Buckeye Trail route goes leisurely up two river valleys to the ridge top. Our alternate route involves a steep road climb out of the Muskingum River Valley, but it is safer. And it's not long before we rejoin the Buckeye Trail.

We're damp from rain and sweat, and as we walk along the ridge, the wind bites through our wet clothing.

This is the most uncomfortable we've been on our hike.

Putting on rain pants at the start of the rain this morning would have been prudent, but the wind did not makes its presence felt until after we were wet. I'm always looking for ways to reduce gear weight, but this rain event makes me decide to keep my nine-ounce rain pants for the duration of the hike. Beth is considering either buying a rain skirt or using something as simple as a 55-gallon trash bag for a protective skirt.

For now, we focus on the promise of a warm shower and dry bed at the Stockport Mill Inn. That goal keeps us moving forward.

Our last county road, McCoy Ridge, descends to State Route 376, and we get our first magnificent view of the Stockport Mill Inn. It is a lovely vista, across a plowed field and the Muskingum River to green wooded hillsides beyond. We feel as if we're walking into a calendar scene of a quaint New England town.

Crossing the bridge over the Muskingum River, we note the locks below, built long ago but still in use for recreational boaters. At 2 p.m., we thankfully enter the B&B and check into Room 207.

The mill has been beautifully restored, maintaining the massive timbers and wooden flooring throughout. The water turbine is now used to generate all the electricity for the bed and breakfast and its associated restaurant.

I am happily hanging up and spreading out all my gear to dry when the lady from the front desk stops in to say that she has made an error and we are to be in Room 206. While 206 has an equally beautiful view, it is slightly smaller and I do not have a table for writing. We dutifully move everything over, though, and settle in for the next two nights.

We make five-o'clock dinner reservations. We both shower (*oh, it feels so good!*), clean up, and feel ready to relax with a leisurely dining experience overlooking the dam, locks, and Muskingum River, which is flowing higher than normal. Beth has a stir-fry vegetable dish on homemade pasta, more vegetables than pasta. I have chicken, potato, and vegetables. We are so satisfied that there is no room for dessert! Our waitress is in her second year at Hocking College, studying wildlife biology. She plans to complete one more semester and then transfer to West Virginia University for a four-year degree. She is delightful to talk with and enthusiastic about her studies.

Even though the B&B is full for tonight, we are the only people in the restaurant, and we relax even more in the spacious surroundings.

Beth enjoys a hot soak in the tub, and we're ready for a good night's rest. Instead of birds singing us to sleep tonight, we'll have the sound of water rushing over the dam.

Day 24: May 15, Sunday

Zero day! And we feel we've earned it!

Breakfast at the B&B is a casual, light affair at our convenience. Our hosts have left a tea cake and hard-boiled eggs in the refrigerator. There are also bananas, apples, and trail mix bars—I haven't had one of those in … let's see … 14 hours.

Outside, the temperature is in the 30-degree range, so we are happy to spend our time indoors, writing notes for the journal and databook, reviewing hiking plans, and reading.

The restaurant opens at noon for a Sunday buffet, which has a substantial selection of salad fixings, meats, casseroles, potatoes, vegetables, and a good variety of desserts. It is a real delight for a hiker's hunger.

Stockport Mill Inn

In mid-afternoon, we walk through Stockport (population 500) on our way to a laundry facility at a nearby campground.

The town was laid out in 1839 and named after a town in England of the same name. The Stockport Mill is the most prominent building in the town. Built in 1842, the mill burned a few years later and was rebuilt in 1849. It was used for 54 years before it burned down a second time, in 1903. The Dover Brothers built the present Stockport Mill in 1906 and two years later fitted the mill with a hydroelectric generator which supplied electricity for 12 village street lights and for grinding Gold Bond pastry flour and Pride of the Valley bread flour.

The mill survived the Great Flood of 1913. In 1928, the hydroelectric operation was shut down when the Suburban Power Company was given the lighting contract for the town. In 1997, new owners renovated the mill into an inn featuring 14 guest rooms with private balconies overlooking the beautiful Muskingum River. And in 2006, the mill's long-silent turbines (which had been refurbished) began generating enough power for the inn and restaurant, with the excess being sold back to American Electric Power.

Stockport Mill Restaurant

The Muskingum River has served as a natural transportation corridor for thousands of years. The herds of elk that once roamed the river valley prompted Native Americans to name the river Moos-kin-gung, which means *Elk Eye River*. Wyandotte and Delaware tribes established towns on the upper Muskingum, but the lower reaches, where elk and bison flourished, were left as hunting grounds.

THE WILDERNESS LOOP

Using flatboats and keelboats, early settlers used the river to transport salt, flour, pork, and apples. Upstream travel required that the crewmen pull or use long, sturdy poles to guide the boats. A round trip between Zanesville and Pittsburgh (down the Muskingum, up the Ohio, and then back) took three to five weeks.

The invention of the steamboat in the early 1800s required that dams be built to create navigable pools over the rocky shallows and tumbling rapids of the Muskingum. Locks were built to lift or lower boats safely around the dams. Steamboat designs then had to be modified so that the boats would fit through the narrow channels of the locks. The paddle wheels on either side of the "side-wheeler" steamboats were replaced by a single wheel on the back of the craft, which then became known as a "sternwheeler." Construction of 11 dams, 12 locks, and 5 side-cut canals on the Muskingum River was completed in 1841.

After our clothes are clean and dry, we make a stop at Windsor Store to purchase food for the next couple of days. The cashier is so pleased with our adventure that she throws in some free flour tortillas. Back in our room, we repack our backpacks and sit back and make ourselves at home. Tomorrow will be another day on the trail.

Chapter 4

LOST TRAIL

Day 25: May 16, Monday
We are up in the common area for our breakfast at 5:45 a.m. Rosetta, a Mennonite, has made a breakfast bun covered with a delicious caramel walnut frosting. The other guests last night were motorcyclists who are taking a four-day course on riding safety. The instructor brings a different group here several times a year. This group ranges in age from 50 to 60; they're from all over the eastern United States and are professors, retired professionals, or business owners—not your typical biker crowd!

We are back in the room when Beth says, "Look out the door!"

The frosty morning has created a vapor cloud as the water tumbles down the dam, and the pre-dawn light gives the top of the plume a reddish-orange glow. We catch the special sight just at the right time.

Bundling up against the 33-degree air, we set out at 6:20. The morning is clear, crisp, and calm as the sun creeps over the horizon. Despite the cold, it is a beautiful, pleasant start to our day's hike.

We walk out of town on sidewalks, passing frost-covered lawns. The trail soon warms us up as we ascend on a road out of the Muskingum River Valley. We startle four deer that were enjoying a peaceful breakfast along a power line right-of-way. Nearing the top of a hillside, we have a last picturesque view back toward Stockport.

After reaching the ridge, the trail descends on a footpath to cross Scott Run. The water is low enough that we can "rock-hop" across.

On the other side, we find a metal box attached to a post; the box contains a trail register. Why the register is here, I do not know, but we take time to sign the register and include the start date of our Buckeye Trail thru-hike.

Trail Register

The trail continues along Scott Run, crossing it a second and a third time. At the third crossing, I have to add a couple of stones in the channel to make rock-hopping possible. It's obvious from the bent plants and gravel deposits along the sides of the stream that just a short time ago we would not have been able to cross it so easily.

We flush out a wild turkey that crashes through the trees as it attempts to fly away.

Back on the road, we see that the sun has begun to melt the frost from the grass. The day is remarkably calm, cloudless, and beautiful—a glorious morning.

A lady on horseback stops and asks if we are hiking the Buckeye Trail. She knows of the trail because it not only goes past her property but at one time went through it.

"Have you seen many hikers?" we ask.

"No, not for a few years," she answers.

When we mention we live on Guilford Lake in northeast Ohio, amazingly, she knows of the lake. She goes to a horse show at Stone Gate Farm, just a couple of miles from Guilford Lake, and afterwards uses the Guilford Lake Campground facilities to sneak a shower.

Just before the town of Chesterhill, the trail goes by a gas station food mart—a convenient stop for an ice tea, soda, and a few minutes' rest. The day remains so beautiful, with a blue sky and warm sunshine, that we plan to do as many miles as we can. The forecast for tomorrow predicts much wetter weather.

Covered Bridge near Chesterhill

Henmen Road out of Chesterhill is a gravel road and runs next to a stream cascading over a rocky bottom. About 0.8 mile down this road, someone has created a rest stop and campsite for BT hikers. A bench has been provided, and there's a flat area that would be large enough for a tent.

Turning onto Thomas Road, we climb upwards, next to a steep, rocky ravine. The ravine is deep and quite spectacular; it would be worthy of designation as a township or county park.

At our turn onto Hoffman Road, we see a sign posted on a tree: DRY WEATHER ROAD. Given the wet weather conditions over the past couple of weeks, this warning sounds ominous.

The sign is accurate—we have to ford a stream twice. We rock-hop the first crossing. At the second ford, I find a log to drop across the water, and we successfully "log-walk" over the stream.

We were told by the BTA that Hoffman Road would take us within a few hundred yards of a campsite by a pond, but we do not find a spur trail or see any evidence of a camping area.

On Newburn Road, we face another concrete depression running under a stream. We take off our shoes and socks to wade across. I put on my sandals for the crossing, and afterward, continue to walk in them. About the time my feet have dried, there is another concrete stream crossing. Already prepared, I wade on through and again walk until my feet are dry. When I am certain there are no more crossings, I put my shoes back on. Beth, on the other hand, is able to easily slip her shoes and socks off and on and does it for both crossings.

Near mile 21 of our day, we arrive at the home of Pete and Marge, who rent a cabin and a campsite to hikers. The rustic cabin has no electricity and just a privy; it rents for $15 per night per person. Tent camping, I believe, is free of charge. We take the time to sit down in their yard while Pete graciously fills our water bottles. He is from upstate New York and has backpacked in the Adirondacks, but he's lived in this area for many years now, managing an orchard. The orchard is hard work, though, and he is finding the beef industry to be easier and more lucrative. His herd is grass fed, so he is knocking down apple trees for more pasture.

Except for short walks on the busier state roads, we have hiked nearly the entire day on the country roads, with only a township dump truck passing us. During the five-o'clock "rush hour," a school bus and perhaps four or five cars go by.

Our hiking funds are now at an even $1.00; Beth and I each found a penny today.

We veer slightly off the official trail to walk by a bed and breakfast on Miller Road. My curiosity is gathering more information for the BT databook.

Then continuing onto State Route 78, we are almost back on the Buckeye Trail when a man pulling a type of brush hog behind his lawn tractor swings up a lane near the highway. Immediately, he stops the mower and introduces himself as Russ Tippett, a member of the Buckeye Trail Association.

We have a long conversation with Russ. He has stories to tell about building a houseboat from an old pontoon and logging nearly 5,000 river miles on it—most notably, the entire Ohio and Missouri Rivers. Though he retired from teaching at Hocking Technical College, he has worn the hat of a game warden and has had other careers. He is now working with disadvantaged kids in an outreach leadership program.

Our conversation lasts long enough to force us to ask if we can camp on his property tonight. He is happy to accommodate us and continues with his stories as we set up our tent.

At Russ's invitation, we go up to the front of his house to admire the stunning panorama from his hilltop domain. He nostalgically recalls that when he was 11 years old he took a ride with his grandmother into town. Stopping on the hilltop to have their sandwiches, he was so impressed with the view that he said, "This will be mine one day." Many years later, his desire came true. And the view is truly marvelous—a rolling, tree-covered landscape, stretching for miles. It is an interesting coincidence that we have camped on private yards twice, and both times we have heard a story about a property capturing a young person's imagination and becoming a dream—a dream that, eventually, becomes reality.

The evening sky is brushed with mares' tails, indicating a change in weather. Since we hiked nearly 25 miles today, we have only 11 miles tomorrow to reach Burr Oak Lodge, our next stop.

Russ tells us a whippoorwill will sing us to sleep, and it does.

Day 26: May 17, Tuesday

We wake to the calls of birds and a very light splattering of rain on the tent. Fortunately, the rain is not enough to wet the tent, and we pack up and are on the BT by 6:40 a.m. The morning is gray, but dry.

Another trail register stands along the path as we head into the woods of Burr Oak State Park. I sign again, writing that our thru-hike started at Lake Erie on April 22 and that our trail names are "Kayak" and "Wildflower."

Hikers generally adopt trail names on long-distance hikes, and the names are an important and interesting part of the hiking culture. Often a trail name is given to a hiker for something they did or said on the trail. A repetitive action, personality quirk, or comical incident all make for great trail-name fodder. A guy who snores loudly may find himself tagged with the name of Chainsaw. If you wait to have a trail name bestowed upon you, don't do something dumb—or you may find that you need a good sense of humor!

Other hikers control their trail-name destiny and give themselves a moniker before beginning the hike. The adopted name may represent an accomplishment, a passion, a family-outing incident, or any other characteristic. Introducing yourself early with a self-chosen trail name precludes the problem of being called something you may not like!

Either way, there is usually an interesting story behind each trail name, and it makes for great conversation. Some trail names we've encountered over the years are Night Train (he hikes at night), Spaceman and Rocket (a couple who works at NASA), Lady Bug, Lady Pants, Storm, Cheetah, Rainbow, Sunshine, Grey Wolf, Silver Fox, Birdman, Thumper, Gonzo, Pancake, Mammoth, Calf, Oz, and Chatty Cathy.

I chose my trail name, Kayak, for two reasons. Over 30 years' time, I have, off and on, raced kayaks. The exercise and conditioning boosted my confidence when I decided to hike the 2,285 miles of the Appalachian Trail at age 59. Also, I believed this trail name would be a unique, simple name to remember on the trail.

Beth arrived at her name after much discussion during our western hikes. We considered what she liked and what name would suit her as she hiked a wilderness trail. As a child, she spent every moment she could outdoors and was also known to defy her parents' guidance. Her brother described her as a "wild flower," explaining that wildflowers thrive in open fields and, brought indoors, wilt quickly. The trail name seems appropriate for Beth.

We finally have our first encounter with other hikers. They are from Virginia and Ohio, are camped at the trailhead to Wildcat Hollow, and plan to hike a 20-mile loop in the area.

Shortly after we part company with the hikers, we find ourselves at the East Branch stream and have no bridge to cross. We take off our socks and shoes, put on sandals, and wade once more. On the other side, we reverse the process and set off again.

Stream Crossing

This part of the trail is muddy, and plenty of poison ivy keeps us on high alert. However, as we hike farther, the tree cover increases; and within two or three miles, the poison ivy is less and the trail is drier. Here the path is fairly well traveled and relatively easy to hike.

This is perhaps one of the most beautiful sections we have been on to date. It may be the first trail segment where a hiker can sit on rocks and enjoy a view. The trail goes along ravines and passes rock cliffs and boulders. Footbridges cross streams and long boardwalks traverse muddy or swampy terrain.

Burr Oak Boardwalk

By 12:30 p.m., we complete our 11-mile hike and arrive at Burr Oak Lodge, check in, take a shower, and head to the lodge restaurant for lunch. We each have veggie burgers and fries; I add a salad to mine and a Klondike bar for dessert.

I spend a few hours preparing an email review of the portion of the Stockport Section which we just completed and then study our schedule for the upcoming days. Tomorrow night, we'll be near Murray City, where the American Legion has given hikers permission to camp on the ball fields overseen by their organization. The next night we will camp in the Wayne National Forest, wherever a campsite is found. For the third night (Friday night), I make a call, hoping to reserve a room at a bed and breakfast.

The lady at the B&B is very cordial and helpful. She explains that she and her husband rent cabins with a two-night minimum stay and they have shut down the B&B portion of their operation. However, when I explain that we are thru-hiking the Buckeye Trail, she becomes interested in helping us and says that we can have the former B&B room for one night, though breakfast will not be included.

We are thrilled with this offer and look forward to meeting her and her husband. They sound like people who have lived interesting lives.

For dinner at Burr Oak Lodge, Beth and I both order pollock, baked potato, and green beans. I, of course, add strawberry shortcake—scrumptious!—and top that off with another Klondike bar.

We then stop at the gift shop and buy out most of their snacks in order to resupply for the next few days of our hike.

Our short hiking day has quickly been filled with chores. At 9:55, it is way past hiker midnight.

Day 27: May 18, Wednesday

This morning I call Sue and Brad to verify arrangements for meeting near Logan or the Old Man's Cave area in a few days.

We check out of the lodge and start hiking around 7:40 a.m. It rained last night, and once again everything is dripping wet and the trails are muddy as we head out under an overcast sky. We slip-slide along the trail—a theme that has been repeated many times. Every intermittent stream has water flowing in it, but the rivulets are small and we hop over or rock-hop each of them. A rocky outcrop, approximately 30 feet high, has a trickle of water tumbling over it.

The trail away from the lodge follows the contours of the land more closely than the trail we followed into the lodge, and today it provides more lake views.

All trees are now in full leaf. The oaks and sycamores seem to be the last to unfurl their leaves. Brilliant red fire pink and yellow buttercups brighten the path, and there is a new, lovely flower—the purplish-blue spiderwort. We pass over a salamander which must be cold; it doesn't want to move when we touch it. Woodpeckers are busy in the distance, and Beth spots a hawk flying among the trees. A box turtle is hanging out on the trail. *Gnarly, dude.*

We start off dry, but slowly the wet grass and bushes soak our lower pants and shoes. Out in the open, away from the protection of the trees, we feel the cool breeze and put our coats back on.

By noon, the cloud layer begins to break; and any time we emerge from the forest paths, we are rewarded with the warmth of the sun. The sun quickly dries our pants, but our feet, unfortunately, stay wet. The day remains cool, making it more comfortable to keep walking than to sit and take a break.

Our bodies seem to have adjusted to the continuous walking, though to sit in the sun on a hilltop with a spacious view would be nice now and then. For now, our motivation is the anticipation of eating our next hot meal and resting at a campsite.

Beth notes that this hike is damp and humid, conditions unfamiliar to her. Her previous experiences hiking in the western mountains have been in the summer, with a high-altitude sun and dry air. We began this hike in the spring, and while we have been fortunate enough to avoid hiking in major storms, the humidity and dampness is a mental challenge for Beth. My expectations of this walk were at least tempered by my experience on the Appalachian Trail.

With these damp thoughts weighing on us, we follow the Buckeye Trail off of Oakdale Road onto an old township road that enters Wallace H. O'Dowd Wildlife Area.

And that is when our day takes a turn for the worse.

The first 0.1 mile is on an old gravel road which ends at a gate. From there, the trail is an ATV track, and a couple of blue blazes clearly indicate which direction to go. A blue blaze by an old oil tank directs us onward. The ATV track has deep ruts filled with water, and large pools—not just puddles—make progress more challenging. It is amazing that ATVs can make it through these areas; it seems almost impossible for a hiker.

LOST TRAIL

After hiking another 45 minutes, I become increasingly concerned that we have not seen a blue blaze since the oil tank. What to do?

We still hope for a blaze or landmark, and so we venture farther.

Finally, I pull out my cell phone, have coverage, and call the BTA office to ask if the trail through the wildlife area is blazed. They mention the oil tank but offer little more than to say the trail is blazed.

But we are standing in the woods and not seeing a blaze.

We must have missed it. We retrace our steps back to the oil tank.

We search for another marked trail ... and find none.

It would be a fool's errand to go back into the woods without blue blazes, so we exit the wildlife area where we entered and are soon once again back on Oakdale Road.

Within a quarter mile, we pass a home where a young man, about twenty, is pulling out of the driveway.

We ask him if he is going to Gloucester.

He is.

Would he mind giving us a ride?

He consents, and we happily hop in.

He drives us to Gloucester, a distance of about four miles. In Gloucester, we quickly hitch another ride to Murray City (population 449), our destination for the night. I call the BTA office to let them know that we are okay, but blue blazes are needed to direct a hiker through the wildlife area.

We soon find ourselves at the American Legion, eating outstanding fish and meatloaf sandwiches with fries. The Legion holds a "Queen of Hearts" lottery drawing every Wednesday, and this jackpot has grown to $297,000, their biggest one ever. The place is already packed with people waiting for the eight-o'clock drawing. We don't stick around for the big festivities but head out to the ball field and tonight's campsite at the edge of town.

Day 28: May 19, Thursday

The cool, 40-degree morning air encourages us to sleep in until 6:10 a.m. It takes us only 20 minutes to pack up and head out under a blue sky and peaceful conditions.

However, we are feeling somber. Is it simply that we have a long walk on the west side of the hills and cannot feel the warmth of the sun on this cool morning? Or is it the scenes we pass—homes of people living in poverty?

Our mood brightens a bit when Beth finds a nickel. She is still waiting to find the mother lode—a big wad of bills.

On a road, our pace is fairly even at three miles per hour, but our off-road pace generally slows. On off-road sections, footing is less certain, terrain is more undulating, and streams and wet areas must be negotiated. Occasionally we also lose time when we need to search for a blue blaze, although, other than yesterday's experience in the wildlife area, the blazes have been adequate.

At a road crossing, we find an open, sunny area and hang Beth's sleeping bag from a signpost to let the moisture evaporate from it. This does not take long, and we set off on a footpath, passing May apple blossoms, buttercups, and raspberry-bush blossoms. Hopefully, we will be hiking in an area at the time when raspberry bushes are full of ripe fruit.

We arrive at Lake Tecumseh around 11:30 and hike the quarter mile into the small village of Shawnee (population 655), where the Buckeye Trail Association office is located. Andrew, BTA director, and Richard, map and graphics coordinator, are there and are delighted to see us. We talk about our trail experience to date and ask about this year's Buckeye TrailFest in Zoar, an event we missed while on the trail. We also learn we are currently on three trails: the Buckeye Trail, the North Country Trail, and the American Discovery Trail. The North Country Trail joins the BT near Zoar and exits in the Defiance area. The American Discovery Trail joins the BT near Chesterhill in southeast Ohio and departs around Cincinnati.

We have a wonderful two-hour visit. They order a large pizza, sodas, and sugar cookies, which we all share—but which I probably indulge in the most.

Richard Lutz and Andrew Bashaw at BTA Office in Shawnee

✧ ✧

During our visit at the BTA office, Andrew mentions that we are "hiking under the radar." There are reasons we have not sought out publicity or assistance along the way.

First, my usual approach to a hike is to research and plan so that I (or we, if Beth is with me) can be as self-sufficient as possible. Diversions to towns take time off the trail. In addition—although assistance from others is necessary and welcomed at times—people do have busy lives, and it can be very difficult to set a specific time and place to meet someone along a trail that is not well known.

The second factor is that the purpose of this hike is to test the information we've assembled for the databook and, at the same time, discover what work is still needed along the Buckeye Trail. This is taking more time than I anticipated; conducting and reporting a review of every day requires several hours, and we don't have the luxury of adjusting our schedule to any great extent. We began this hike only days after we returned from a trip abroad, and we want to finish in time to join a week-long family reunion.

The third reason we hike the way we do is that we hike this trail—and others—to find what the trail itself has to offer. When we're dedicated to the trail, we may walk from one point to the next and find we have traveled through centuries. The endeavor may not be possible every day, but I like to seek out hints of other time periods. The trail takes us not only through other eras, but also through other worlds—we are seeing the worlds of hawks and box turtles and rushing waters and forest wildflowers.

Every hiker will experience the trail differently. There will be different encounters, varying weather conditions, and individual timetables, but the trail always has something to offer.

However, the downside of traveling self-sufficiently and under the radar is that publicity would undoubtedly benefit the BTA, and, we remind ourselves, that is also one of the goals of our thru-hike of the Buckeye Trail.

We snap photos of ourselves with Andrew and Richard by the BTA office sign, say goodbye, and proceed back to the trail.

The four miles of trail to our campsite is blazed, but at a fork in the trail, we take about 10 minutes to locate a blaze to point us in the right direction. The section also has a lot of poison ivy, which gives thought to how nice a shower would be tonight. However, our primitive campsite at the Old Stone Church Hollow Trailhead does not have such amenities.

The trailhead received its name from the arched-wall ruins of St. Peter's Catholic Church (circa 1845), located just north of this site. During the Civil War, the area mined iron ore from these hills to make cannonballs for the Union Army. Now the church ruins and 102 gravestones are all that remain of the once-thriving community. One version of local history has the people moving to nearby New Straitsville, where another Catholic church was built in 1871.

We neglected to refill our water bottles at the BTA office, and we drank more than expected on the way to our campsite. Fortunately, I have cell-phone coverage and contact Richard at the BTA office; he is planning to stop by later, and I ask him to bring a gallon of water.

Cell phones are so commonly used now that we take them for granted; however, coverage is not universal. I have Verizon, which has generally provided better coverage on the Buckeye Trail than Beth's AT&T coverage, but we did find spots where AT&T gave us coverage and Verizon did not.

Richard arrives at our camp around 5 p.m., and we spend another hour talking about trail experiences. He is doing more hiking and has several questions for us. He also has experiences of his own to share.

We have spent four full weeks hiking the Buckeye Trail. When we camped at Murray City last night, we had completed approximately one-third of our walk around Ohio.

Trail Notes

Chapter 5

OHIO'S GEM

Day 29: May 20, Friday
Before I fell asleep last night, I heard an owl hoot twice. I heard it again this morning. Turkeys are gobbling in the distance, too.

We take 35 minutes to pack up and start down the trail at 6:36, with a thin veil of mist filtering the sunlight. Within five minutes we are at a stream. Fortunately, the torrential flow indicated by the bent grasses higher on the stream bank has subsided enough that we can rock hop across after I add one rock. The weather recently has been drier; and as the woods dry out, the low, wet areas of the trail can be negotiated with greater ease and we can move faster.

The trail is well maintained, so poison ivy is not an issue today. In addition, much of the 7-mile section of woodland trail this morning appears to have been rebuilt recently. Machines were obviously used, as well as tons of gravel.

The trail follows a ridgeline, and so it's relatively flat. On this section, a hiker will do well to simply enjoy the walk and not look too closely at the map. The trail twists and turns, advancing us westward only two miles.

Griggs Road is a refreshingly pleasant road to walk. Paved and lightly traveled, it runs beside a stream that tumbles over a rocky bottom in a series of little waterfalls, pools, and cascading riffles. The trees are near, but breaks in the green tunnel allow occasional views of the slowly thickening vapor layer in the sky. As we continue our ascent, the stream peters out. The ridgetop offers no views as we pass over—the trees are tall and in full leaf.

We cross a state highway and continue to make our way toward Bear Run Road, where, upon arriving at 1:15 p.m., we divert from the BT to hike or hitch to Bear Run Bed & Breakfast. To anyone who still thinks road walks are too risky due to traffic: We hike the entire 2.3 miles with only one car passing us—and that vehicle was going in the opposite direction. However, that also means that we have had no chance for hitchhiking.

At 2 p.m., we meet Phil Myers, who is mowing by the Bear Run entrance gate. Phil—also known as "Bud"—is 78 years old, and we have a delightful time chatting with him about the couple's eight years of missionary work in the Philippines.

During their time there, Phil had a hiking adventure of his own. Friends had asked if he would like to go on a hike, but little did he know what he would encounter while hiking in a tropical environment. Leeches were one of several unpleasant surprises. A washed-out bridge prevented them from reaching the plane that was to take them out of the wilderness. They spent the night in a little village close to the bridge, and during the night, one partner became sick with dysentery and they were all severely bitten by bedbugs. The next day, they solved the bridge problem by asking the Filipinos to cut a few trees and let them fall across the ravine. The plan worked, and they had a bridge to the airport.

Up at the house, we meet Phil's wife, Marcia. She has designed beautiful flower beds around the house, and peonies and glorious irises are in full bloom. She also does "Sculpey" sculpting. Her characters are similar to the caricature drawings that artists do of people at street fairs, and she has created a baker, wash lady, toymaker, Santa flight coordinator, doll maker, a modern Santa, and a historic Santa—and she has plans for still more.

Our hosts invite us to join them for stir-fried shrimp, but their home loses power before cooking commences. We learn there's a tree across a power line somewhere, so we order a pizza.

At dinner, more stories are shared. During Phil and Marcia's missionary work in the Philippines, a person came to them with a child with a cleft lip. Phil found a means for the boy to see a plastic surgeon who did the procedure for only a $20 charge for anesthetics. From this small beginning grew a worldwide organization to help children needing the same surgery.

Phil and Marcia returned to their Ohio farm, and he ministered in Lancaster, Ohio, then switched to construction work. They launched the B&B and cabin-rental business 25 years ago. Through this enterprise, they've met many people, even hosting Joan Baez and her traveling entourage as guests. Our evening conversation with them was relaxing—and kept us up an hour past our hiker midnight.

Day 30: May 21, Saturday

Again, we are glad to have spent the night indoors—our hosts mention that the area received an inch of rain overnight. Rain has made it a difficult month for farmers; it's been too wet to work the fields, either plowing or making hay. We enjoy our comfort and make it a lazy, easy-going morning by sleeping in until 7 a.m.

Breakfast is at 7:45, and Marcia prepares eggs, toast, and a bowl of fruit. Breakfast was not to be included in our sleeping arrangement, but they apparently enjoy our company and are delighted to have us join them for breakfast.

They are not finished with doing favors for us and insist on taking us back to the Buckeye Trail. As he drives us back, Phil describes the boundaries of his land; we pass his alpacas and horses; and he talks about the 40 head of cattle he recently sold off. We divert a short distance to see his childhood home and a concrete-block structure for milking that he built at the age of 15. It still looks in good condition, though the barn next to it is now gone. Our time with Phil and Marcia turned out to be so enjoyable, and we thank them for opening up their home to us.

The BT follows a road, and we pass the entrance to Camp Akita, the site of the 2014 Buckeye TrailFest that Beth and I attended two years ago, when we volunteered to work on the databook project. Later we pass by Crockett's Run, another place a person can rent a cabin right on the Buckeye Trail. (Crockett's Run also has a two-night minimum stay policy.)

The entrance to our off-road section crosses over a beautiful stream next to a moss-covered sandstone formation rising about 15 feet—topped off with hemlock trees growing on its crown.

In Logan (population 7,152), we check into the Baymont Inn, conveniently located near a Walmart store, an antique store, Olde Dutch Restaurant, and other little shops. A bonus for us is that the hotel is next to Fox's Canoe Livery. Tomorrow we hope to rent a canoe for an easy, 7-mile paddle that passes a natural rock bridge. At Walmart, we purchase enough trail mix, cheese, tortillas, protein bars, and crackers for five days.

At the Baymont Inn, I notice a wall display with historical information about Logan. The city was founded by then-Governor Thomas Worthington in 1816 and named after Chief Logan of the Mingo tribe. As in many other towns along the canal corridors of Ohio, businesses flourished with the increased traffic brought by the canal. In addition, rich deposits of coal were discovered in the area; iron ore was mined for weapons during the Civil War; and the clay soils gave rise to the manufacture of clay products. All of these resources made it possible for the town of Logan to survive, even after the canal ceased operation and local coal mines declined and closed.

Today we walked the New Straitsville Section of the BT. As we complete each of the Buckeye Trail sections, I write up comments for the databook and send them to the BTA office. The additional work adds a little stress to the hike and limits time we could spend on more relaxing pursuits. However, our hope is that the databook becomes a valuable asset for BT hikers.

Day 31: May 22, Sunday

Morning dawns bright and promising, but Ohio clouds soon move in for a morning that has only partial sunshine. We have a leisurely breakfast at the inn and at 9:30 go next door to Fox's Hocking Hills Canoe Livery, where we catch the ten-o'clock canoe shuttle.

By 10:20, we are floating down the Hocking River, moving without heavy packs on our backs or the use of our legs. The river is moving faster than normal because of the recent rains, and so the trees and scenery flow by with little effort on our part.

We're soon at the stop for the natural rock bridge and, after securing the canoe, we walk about 400 feet to the sandstone formation. The arch, considered the largest natural feature of its kind in Ohio, is approximately 50 feet high and spans a ravine about 150 feet wide. The stream which created this formation provides a waterfall behind the rock bridge, and the flowing water seems to bring the place alive.

Once again in the canoe, we pass moss-covered sandstone cliffs with recesses etched into them by the river. Several turtles solemnly observe us floating by. We were told to look for otters, but only spot three riverbank mud slides where otters may have moved in and out of the water. A blue heron greeted us at the start of the trip, and one bids us goodbye as we near our take-out at 12:40.

Back at the Baymont Inn, we meet up with my sister and brother-in-law, Sue and Brad, who have driven down to join us for the hike through the gorgeous and popular Hocking Hills area tomorrow.

Before starting today's hike, we gladly turn over our backpacks to Sue and Brad. In a long distance hike, the term *slackpacking* is used for hiking farther down the trail without carrying a backpack. This generally occurs when someone else can move your pack to your next destination, as Sue and Brad will do for us today. We will meet them at the Old Man's Cave Visitor Center.

Wildcat Hollow Road wends its way around beautiful rock outcrops and overhanging trees with grand canopies reaching over and touching each other. The narrow road has the feeling of a woodland trail, and no traffic disrupts the serenity.

When we leave Big Pine Road and start down a footpath, our world turns magical. A bridge arches over a creek that winds its way between tree-lined banks. Leaf-filtered sunlight sparkles on the water. Within a quarter mile of climbing through the forest, we arrive at the base of massive sandstone cliffs, ledges, and boulders. This is a grand prelude to the spectacular natural wonders we know are waiting for us in the Hocking Hills Section.

A trail leads along the base of massive rock cliffs; it beckons, calling us to see what majestic sights it has to offer. However, the blue blazes lead in the opposite direction, up through a narrow passage in the cliff wall, as if passing through some massive gate. We follow the blue blazes, and on top, we look down and see one formation that stands out—a broad rock sitting perhaps 30 feet up on a narrow rock column. It's called "The Balancing Rock."

The trail winds around and crosses a stream so small that it may be dry in summer. When there is an opening in the vegetation, we can look back and see that the stream is falling over a tall, horseshoe-shaped ledge. The lower section of the cliff has eroded, creating a huge, open-faced cave. Trees grow up to the edge of the ledge and prevent us from photographing the grand natural feature, and no trail seems to lead down to its base.

Opposite Page: The Balancing Rock

OHIO'S GEM

The final feature in this magical land of rocks, cliffs, and trees is the Big Spring. Water flows out of the hillside with such volume as to create an instant stream just a few feet from a ledge, where it spills over as a magnificent waterfall.

Our breath has been taken away—not from any difficult climb, but by the unexpected grandeur of this walk.

Shortly after the Big Spring, logging activities have removed all the trees—and, hence, all the blue blazes. We choose a path through the open area and eventually cross a road. We consult the BT map, locate the position where the BT officially crosses the road (about a half mile away), and rejoin the BT there.

Our final couple of miles to the Hocking Hills Park office is more sedate, up and down, through the forest terrain. We meet Sue and Brad, who transport us to a cabin they have rented in the state park, giving us another comfortable bed, a delicious dinner, and conversation with family. Sue has baked a rhubarb pie for dessert. We put three candles in the pie, in celebration of Beth's 63rd birthday.

It's a joyful end to a good day.

Day 32: May 23, Monday
Today the four of us enter one of the jewels of Ohio—the stunning beauty of the Old Man's Cave Gorge. The trail starts near a plaque dedicated to Emma "Grandma" Gatewood on January 17, 1981. The plaque reads as follows:

> Grandma Gatewood Memorial Hiking Trail.
> This six-mile trail is dedicated to the memory of Grandma Gatewood, a vibrant woman, seasoned hiker, and longtime Hocking Hills enthusiast. The path begins here, visits Cedar Falls, and terminates at Ash Cave.

OHIO'S GEM

Grandma Gatewood Plaque and Trail

In 1955, at the age of 67, Emma Gatewood thru-hiked the Appalachian Trail, becoming the first woman to do so, and repeated the hike in 1960. She was one of the founding members of the Buckeye Trail Association.

The Buckeye Trail follows the Grandma Gatewood Trail, descending into the gorge, and we are surrounded by 30 feet or more of sandstone cliffs covered in mosses and ferns, with large hemlock trees growing up wherever they can find a foothold, be it on ground, boulders, or even the side of a cliff.

The sandstone rock of the gorge began to form 400 million years ago when the region was a shallow sea. For 100 million years, sand and gravel washed down from surrounding ancient mountains. Then, 300 million years ago, the land began to rise and the sea retreated. Erosion over the next couple hundred million years carved the cliffs, caves, and waterfalls that make up the Hocking Hills region.

The only sad part of our walk through the spectacular gorge is that, looking closely, we can see that the hordes of visitors have trampled the earth, compressing it and destroying all new growth.

What will happen when the old trees die and are gone? Will the transformation of the area be so slow that each new generation will not realize what has been lost? We encourage people to come and enjoy, but stay on the path. (Hocking Hills is one of only four Ohio state parks that actually have a law stating no one is permitted off the posted trails.) More boardwalks, railings, and steps are needed to protect the trail, tree roots, and landscape. The people of tomorrow rely on our respect for nature today!

Upper Falls – Old Man's Cave

But today we can enjoy the many trickles of water seeping from dozens of cracks and layers of stone, feeding the cliff plants and adding cool moisture to the gorge. The trickles also feed the main stream running through the gorge and the many waterfalls along its course. Arched stone bridges and restraining walls, built decades ago, are now covered in their own layers of moss and ferns. People who have the good fortune of passing through after a rain will have a greater reward—water carved the gorge, and water gives it life.

Today we meet more people walking than we have on our entire hike to date. This area is not to be rushed; there is too much to take in and admire in nature's handiwork.

As we hike beyond the Old Man's Cave area, we leave the masses of people behind and begin to see what former beauty existed in the gorge. The trail narrows, and flowers and other plants grow up to its edge. The leaf litter gives the soil richness and softness, allowing for a wider variety of plants and a foothold for new shrubs and trees. The trail passes through stands of large hemlocks and sycamores. Sunlight filters through the trees in brilliant shafts of light.

The woods of southern Ohio are only a small remnant of what the first frontiersmen saw when they entered the territory that would become Ohio. The magnificent virgin forest was so extensive that it is said a squirrel could climb a tree in Pennsylvania and travel all the way to Indiana without coming down to the ground. The early settlers regarded this forest as a dismal place, though, and by 1900, the once expansive forest was reduced to less woodland than is seen today. Fortunately, the forest has been allowed to make a small comeback.

We join up with a small stream that will cascade over an immense ledge 700 feet wide, 100 feet deep, and 90 feet tall—and Ash Cave provides a grand finale for today's spectacular walk.

Ash Cave received its name from the ashes covering its floor, the accumulated remains of countless campfires of the Native Americans who used the shelter for untold centuries. The cave was also a meeting place for them; the cavern forms a natural amphitheater, offering a venue for speeches, a place where many individuals could gather and hear one person's voice.

The trail is then back on roads leading away from this gorgeous area. But the roads are one lane and tree lined; and, with each ascent and descent, the road passes through the sandstone which gives the area its many cliffs.

Brad has been the generous person who has gone back on the trail periodically to move the car forward; and as the four of us end our slackpack hike, we can now enjoy a ride back to our cabin for dinner, a shower, and a comfortable bed.

Chapter 6

TICKS AND SOUTHERN OHIO

Day 33: May 24, Tuesday
After a good breakfast with Sue and Brad, we load up our backpacks and we're driven back to our drop-off point. I am carrying food for five days because we are not certain where we will be able to resupply in the next segment—the Scioto Trail Section—of the hike.

Sue and Brad walk with us awhile, and at Lady Run Road, a closed, unmaintained township road, we find that it is now a narrow ATV trail. ATVs have essentially created a ditch down the hillside, and there's water flowing through it. The ATVs turn up the dirt; and then the stream and rain create mud, which slowly erodes away. Sections are so deeply eroded that the forested sides are now nearly seven feet above what was once the road.

Brad and Sue hike part way up the hill with us before deciding it is time for them to return to their car. We thank them again for coming out and adding a sprinkle of joy to our hike.

Crossing over the ridgetop, we find the road is a better, one-lane "trail," and we eventually turn onto a paved, open road in the full morning sun.

But in a mile we are again on a one-lane road where the trees press in, completely shading our walk. Along this lane, a low hum can just barely be heard. Cicadas! This is supposed to be a big year with the 17-year cicadas.

Our one-lane road becomes an ATV route again, with the stream winding through it, and we constantly have to step over or through the water and mud. Any place that is not a rock or stone is a muddy mess, eroding away.

Eroded ATV "Ditch"

At 11:20, as we turn onto Clark Hollow Road, a tanker truck comes down the hill to the stop sign. The driver rolls down his window and says, "Still walking? I saw you guys back in Macksburg!" We are stunned and yet excited that our paths cross after so many miles and 10 days. Amazing, what happens on the trail over time.

At Tar Hollow State Park, we enter the woods on a footpath and the beauty is literally underfoot. Our feet are the biggest impact now.

Here the trail uses switchbacks, making it easier to reach the ridgetop and lessening erosion of the hillside. After about an hour, however, we can see the trail and the blue blazes, but as we walk we have to push aside branches, briars, and other forest plants growing over the trail, determined to reclaim the territory.

Soon, we cross logging roads that were recently used and now show a feeble attempt at reseeding with some sort of grass. Here the trail is essentially destroyed. Someone obviously had more interest in money from logging than in maintenance of a scenic buffer for the BT.

We finally lose the blue blazes completely and spend nearly an hour searching for any sign of the trail.

Finally, we give up, and I call the BT section supervisor, Deven Atkinson. He informs us the trail has been closed for two years!

We describe where we are, and he says we need to look for a road with baseball-sized stone on it and a fire tower. He will drive from Waverly and meet us at the fire tower.

We backtrack and find the road and then the fire tower. Deven arrives 15 minutes later.

He tells us there are more logging issues several miles down the trail and suggests we stay on Mr. Detty's property to bypass the damaged trail. After we make a brief stop at a gas station to fill our water bottles, Deven introduces us to Mr. Detty, who is very cordial. His 91st birthday is coming up on July 29, and he served in the Navy during World War II. He shows us land he mows around an old, abandoned house across the street and says we can camp there.

Happy to be out of our dilemma, we hope to continue our hike without further incident. It certainly would be appreciated if the Buckeye Trail could be more protected in areas of logging.

Day 34, May 25, Wednesday

Around midnight, Beth heard an animal making low snorting and screaming sounds at the edge of the woods. A bobcat? Cougar? Bear? I don't know what it sounded like—I slept soundly. Beth kept vigil all night, periodically shining a flashlight toward the woods and the glowing eyes. We will need to buy new batteries.

We stir in the morning light at 5:45 (with no dangerous animal in sight) and head out at 6:20. Our morning hike starts with a steep, 20-minute climb on an unmaintained trail. We have no choice but to whack our way through to the ridgetop, where we join an ATV track.

We again encounter a logging area, but it is only a short section. Next is a long field of dew-covered grass which drenches our feet, a short road walk, and then another dewy pasture for 0.6 mile. Cattle in the pasture seem unperturbed at our passing. As we cross the exit gate, a bull gives us a parting bellow. I hope he said, "Happy trails!"

And then ...

Ticks! Hundreds of them!

During our visit at the BTA office, Richard warned us; he had encountered ticks before and after a concrete hiker's tunnel under State Route 35—but, oh, my gosh, this invasion is overwhelming!

We can move forward just minutes at a time before we must pause and brush dozens of ticks—big ones to tiny red ones—off our clothes.

This goes on for about two miles until we turn onto a logging skid road and seem to have left them behind. But we still spend the next couple of hours checking, and we find them, either tucked away in a fold of clothing or moving about in search of our skin. That is one stretch of the trail we do not wish to revisit during tick season!

Crossing the bridge over the Scioto River, we celebrate a minor milestone. We are approximately 60 miles due south of Columbus.

Hiking into the Scioto Trail State Park campground we find there is water but no showers—and it would be oh, so nice to scrub down after our tick-infested hike. We have seen several ticks before today; hopefully, "several" ticks are all we will encounter on the remainder of the hike.

Day 35: May 26, Thursday

The birds are still reliable alarm clocks; they let us know when it is 5:45. With no growling wild animals, Beth slept much better last night; but we were startled awake when a large branch crashed to the ground. This morning, in the light of dawn, we saw a large oak branch lying across the campground road about 100 yards from us. Thankfully, there was no harm or damage to anyone or anything.

TICKS AND SOUTHERN OHIO

Scioto Trail State Park Campground

We head out at 6:25, in weather that has, in the last couple days, become more hot and humid. Toads are more plentiful along the trail, and the cicadas' low hum is constant.

The trails near Scioto Trails State Park are also bridle trails. Horse traffic keeps the weeds down but apparently is not so heavy that the trail has been degraded for hiking. In parts of southern Ohio, we've found that foot traffic alone is not sufficient to keep brush from reclaiming the trail. We look forward to the time when the trail takes on a worn, well-used look, imparted by the boots and shoes of hiking clubs who take an interest in using and maintain the trail.

Our last off-road section today is about two miles long. The trail is barely visible but well blazed, and we have no problem moving through the woods. Part of the trail follows a tree-shaded fence line through a pasture, and as we approach, two horses abandon their favorite shady hang-out and trot away from us. Curiosity gets the better of them, though; and, sniffing the air, they move cautiously toward the strange, humpbacked creatures. Once they have determined we are only two deformed humans, they relax and become more sociable, escorting us to the end of the pasture.

Other than this encounter, the forested walk is uneventful, and we again come back to a paved road which eventually narrows to one lane and turns to dirt.

We have only a couple of miles to our destination when a pickup truck stops next to us and the friendly driver asks, "Are you hiking the Buckeye Trail?" We find so few people who know about the BT that it shocks us when someone asks that question.

This man was involved with Boy Scouts until his son was finished with scouting. One of their favorite activities was backpacking, and they have done walks on the Buckeye Trail, the Appalachian Trail, and the trails at Camp Philmont in New Mexico. He works in forestry and still enjoys getting out into the woods.

Our destination today is the 180-acre Mapleberry Farm, owned by Gale and Sharon Rickey. The BT goes right past the farm, and the Rickeys enjoy having hikers pitch a tent on their lawn.

Gale welcomes us and tells us about the farm's maple sugaring operation; they made and sold maple syrup for 30 years. Up until a couple of years ago, he tapped over 1,200 sugar maple trees. He loved giving tours to school kids and explaining the process of collecting and boiling the sap. The Rickeys' big farm garden has not yet been completely planted; the area has received so much rain that many people have not been able to work in their gardens.

After showering, we relax, sitting on the porch and in the yard. It's a sunny afternoon with a warm breeze, and this is a delightful respite.

Gale's wife, Sharon, arrives home. She is a director of the WIC (Women, Infants, and Children) supplemental nutrition program for two counties. We order a pizza, and Gale and I head out to pick it up while Sharon and Beth put together a salad and cook fresh asparagus. Sharon has also made a strawberry shortcake! Yum!

During our dinner conversation, I find out that Sharon's senior-year roommate at Ohio University is married to a former plant manager at Cardinal Electric Generating Plant, a man whom I knew when I also worked there. Small world!

It's a late evening, and we do not get into our tent until 9 p.m. We snuggle before falling asleep to the familiar sound of a whippoorwill.

Day 36: May 27, Friday

At 5:50 a.m., we are up. Forty minutes later, we're hiking under a beautiful, cloudless morning sky. There's no breeze, and we soon feel the warmth of the sun.

We pass a historic Baptist Church, established in 1824. Painted white, it is in very good condition and appears to still be in use. A historical marker provides details about those involved with the construction of the church. In summary: In the 1820s, 13 African-American families migrated from Virginia to Peebles, Ohio. Their excellent farming skills allowed them to prosper, a situation which angered their white neighbors who then began a campaign of harassment. Ten of the original families eventually moved away, but other African-Americans continued to arrive and join the settlement. They founded the Eden Baptist Church and organized a school. Several of the families were also involved in the Underground Railroad. By the 1950s, residents had moved to other communities for economic reasons. The marker does not state who is currently attending and maintaining the church.

Our delicious pizza yesterday came from FredNeck's Mini Mart, and the store happens to be on the trail. We arrive at FredNeck's around 8:30, buy ice tea and soft drinks, and spend about an hour catching up on journal notes.

In the woods again, we soon pass a small pond, where a bull frog croaks and splashes in.

Ever since our encounter with the hordes of ticks, the days seem more difficult to get through. A wooded hike in southern Ohio means dealing with ticks, nettles, greenbriers, wild rose, and poison ivy. Maybe it is just a psychological thing and we feel on edge because we are worrying about finding more ticks on our clothes and bodies. Supposedly, ticks are killed by clothing that has been treated with permethrin. Unfortunately, we left our permethrin supply stored safely in our garage. The constant vigilance does add stress to our days.

But we try to look past the difficulties today and admire a beautiful rock ledge rising high to our right and a dry, rocky stream bed to our left. Young sassafras, ash, oak, and beech trees all wait patiently for an opening in the forest canopy where they can grow rapidly to fill the void. We admire ferns, forest bushes, and wildflowers. Birds can be heard all around us in this world of green.

Halfway into our wooded hike, we take a 30-minute break at a picnic table provided by the Pike County Horsemen's Club. The table is situated on a hill with a grand view overlooking a wooded valley.

Picnic Table with View

Of course, we use the opportunity to do a complete tick check and still find them on us and hiding in folds of our clothes. There's nothing to do but pick them all off and continue along the woodland trail toward our goal of Pike Lake State Park campground.

It's Friday afternoon and the start of Memorial Day weekend, but thankfully there are still three sites left in the campground when we arrive at 3 p.m. Surprisingly, this campground has a good store for sandwiches and supplies and, near the beach area—laundry facilities and showers! Campers can also rent paddle boats, kayaks, and canoes.

We eat ice cream while looking out over the park's small but lovely lake. After setting up our tent, we walk to the beach to shower in the changing rooms. Back at our campsite, we wash some clothes and set them in the sun to dry, check our equipment and supplies, write journal notes, check trail maps, and relax a little.

That's life on the trail.

Day 37: May 28, Saturday

We did not fall asleep to the sound of the whippoorwill last night, but to the sounds of humanity descending upon 112 sites at the Pike Lake Campground. Big trucks, RVs, cars, kids running, kids riding all sorts of bikes and trikes, campfires crackling, parents calling to kids, and motors running—hardly a wilderness trail experience. But we did have food, showers, and a safe place to spend the night; and eventually we did sleep, probably well after 9 p.m.

Our arrival at the Pike Lake State Park marked the end of the Scioto Trail Section of the Buckeye Trail. Today, we will begin the Sinking Spring Section. A portion of the trail we will hike today is named after Jim Sprague, in honor of his dedication to and work on the Buckeye Trail. (Jim supplied us with shuttle service when we hiked the Akron Section last fall.)

We are up early, ready for a long day, and on the trail at 6:10 a.m., but within half a mile, our day starts off wrong. We turn onto a bridle trail and have walked another half mile before we realize there are no blue blazes. We're forced to backtrack, and we find the Buckeye Trail 100 feet beyond the bridle trail turnoff.

This section of off-road trail is wider and better maintained, and there seem to be fewer ticks. Nevertheless, to help keep ticks at bay, we have applied Vicks Vapor Rub on our legs near our socks and Deet insect repellant to our pants.

Jim Sprague Trail Sign

Nighttime and early morning temperatures are now in the 60s and daytime temperatures into the 80s, a big change from a few days ago. We no longer start with coats on in the morning, and we welcome shade during the day. We make the most of our stops where there is water, rehydrate in the evening, and drink about 20 ounces before starting out in the morning.

We have seen many tiger swallowtail butterflies and also many beautiful black ones, perhaps spicebush swallowtails. A box turtle on the trail heading our direction says he also started at Headlands Beach on Lake Erie—but his start was 10 years ago!

We pass through a beautiful forest where the floor is covered with ferns. But soon we are two sweaty people ascending a steep hill vertically because there are no switchbacks. Once on the ridgetop, we hit an easier stride and enjoy the good-sized oak, beech, hickory, and maple trees that make up much of the forest.

Conversation with a Turtle

Our descent is on a skid road, and along the way we miss a turnoff that would take us to the Butler Springs Christian Camp, our destination for today. When we intersect with State Route 41, we must bear left for 0.4 mile to correct our direction, and then we cross the BT as we enter the camp.

The camp is rented out to a group having a family reunion, and someone in the group directs us to Chris, who is in charge of the camp. Chris is an avid hiker and has hiked to the summit of 30 state highpoints. His attempts to summit Mount Hood and Mount Rainier were unsuccessful, but he enjoyed the adventure and the challenge of trying. He makes us feel at home and shows us where to do laundry, set up our tent, and shower off the day's sweat.

A gentleman who is trailer camping near us introduces himself as Bob O'Connor. He is an electronics engineer, but also an avid Indian mound enthusiast. He shows us a book entitled *Encyclopedia of Native American Mounds and Earthworks* by Gregory Little. We are captivated as we learn that Ohio has 40,000 mounds and that the biggest mound in the United States is the huge Cahokia site at Collinsville, Illinois.

It is a serendipitous education about Indian mounds—because tomorrow we will follow the Buckeye Trail through the first of three mound systems.

Day 38: May 29, Sunday

We take our time packing up and do not exit the camp until 7:20 a.m. The Fort Hill earthworks are only a few minutes away, and we arrive by 7:35. We diverge from the Buckeye Trail to the Fort Hill trail, which allows us to climb up and across the earthworks.

As we exit Fort Hill, a farm scene spreads out before us. Hay fields, cattle, and hills stand against a dramatic backdrop of dark clouds pierced by rays of sunlight.

We walk into Sinking Spring (population 134) in time to hear the church bells ring for a ten-o'clock service. We buy two days of food at Family Dollar and then go across the street to a gas station food mart to buy tuna sandwiches, V8 drinks, and a banana. The forecast calls for 35 percent chance of rain by 5 p.m. today.

We head out of town and by early afternoon arrive at the Buckeye Trail shelter on the McKenzie property. The structure is on private property, so we call the owners (who live nearby) to request permission to use the shelter for the night. They sound friendly and seemed pleased to be able to help us out on our long journey.

Dropping our packs at the shelter first, we walk about 0.1 mile to a second famous Indian earthwork, the Serpent Effigy Mound.

At the museum, we watch a 10-minute video before walking around this amazing mound. It is thought that the twists in the serpent's body represent directional points to sunrise and moonrise at important times of the year, such as solstices and equinoxes. The summer solstice is said to be over the egg shape at the mouth of the serpent. A historical marker at Serpent Mound reads as follows:

One of North America's most spectacular Effigy Mounds, Serpent Mound is a gigantic earthen sculpture representative of a snake. Built on a spur of rock overlooking Ohio Brush Creek around 1000 A.D. by the Fort Ancient culture, the earthwork was likely a place of ceremonies dedicated to a powerful serpent spirit. The site is located on the edge of a massive crater, possibly formed by the impact of a small asteroid around 300 million years ago. Frederick Ward Putman studied Serpent Mound between 1886 and 1889. Due largely to his efforts, Serpent Mound became the first privately funded archaeological Preserve in the United States.

Serpent Mound

The Indians may not have known the geologic importance of the area. It may have simply been a promontory convenient for their ceremonies. However, it is now known that the serpent effigy sits on the western rim of a five-mile-wide circular crater. Nearly 300 million years of erosion erased the obvious signs of a crater, but scientists studying rock samples from two core drillings in the area have found evidence of shock metamorphism features in quartz grains, as well as the presence of impact-melt rock. Geochemical analyses of impact breccias show minor enrichments in the elements cobalt, chromium, nickel, and iridium which would have come from a meteor impact.

The Serpent Mound crater is the only verified impact crater in the state of Ohio.

It is 3:15 p.m. and 85 degrees. I use more than an hour to catch up on journals in the shade of a picnic shelter. Then it's time to head back to the BT shelter for dinner and sleep.

Shelter

Day 39: May 30, Monday (Memorial Day)

From our shelter last night, we had a grand view of a thunderstorm. The display began around 10:30 p.m. with flashes of lightning and rolling thunder.

Then at 11:30, chaos descended. The shelter's garage-door roof began to leak, and we moved our sleeping bags. A few more leaks developed, and we moved again. More leaks broke, and water began to puddle on the floor. Finally we found a corner of the shelter where we could stay dry.

In addition to the leaking roof, the opening to the shelter is so high that water can spray in from the rain. Conclusion: not the best shelter design. It was, however, our first real thunderstorm on this trip while we were camping, and it was nice to have a front-row seat despite our scurrying to stay dry.

I went back to sleep, but Beth was impressed by the storm and stayed up to enjoy the show. The high opening of the shelter and large, freshly mowed field in front of us provided a tremendous view of the night sky. Before the rains started, the field was full of fireflies. While the storm raged, the fireflies continued flying. How do they do that? The winds were high and the rain drops heavy, but the little guys kept up their show. Lightning flashes would periodically illuminate the entire scene. It seemed to go on for hours but Beth did not want to miss a lightning bolt or clap of thunder. It was another short night for Beth—but this time, a wonderful night.

We have a long day ahead of us, and we are on the trail by 6 a.m. Dark clouds from last night's storm are still scurrying overhead, but a pink glow in the east indicates the dawn of another day and, perhaps, Mother Nature's apology for the violent storm. The sky remains overcast for our early morning road walk into Peebles.

The town of Peebles (population 1,782) traces its history back to the building of the Cincinnati and Eastern Railway across Zane's Trace in 1881. Isaiah Custer lived in the area and donated land for a train depot; this development encouraged others to build houses and businesses. The resulting town became known as Peebles, named after Portsmouth businessman John G. Peebles, who had contributed to the construction of the railroad. The village of Peebles prospered into the early twentieth century, and though it is no longer a railroad "boom town," it still draws shoppers from a wide area.

Peebles is also known for hosting the first chautauqua in Adams County. Chautauquas were week-long road shows, held annually throughout America, that were formatted to be educational, artistic, and entertaining.

The landscape is gradually changing as we walk toward southwestern Ohio. The hills of southeastern Ohio are giving way to a gently rolling countryside and wider valleys. (However, steep inclines are not completely behind us!) We have seen deer on most days on our hike and still hear woodpeckers whenever we pass through a wooded section. Red salamanders are recently new to the scene. We spot another box turtle, a favorite of mine, near the road.

We also hear the mysterious animal scream again—this time, during daylight. After Beth googles animal sounds, we decide it must be a bobcat. Once extirpated from Ohio, bobcats are returning, and sightings are becoming more common.

We have two off-road sections today, each two miles long. The first is on property owned by General Electric Corporation. At the center of about 7,000 acres and away from residential areas, GE tests jet engines, putting new designs through various durability tests of on/off cycles as well as continuous operation. In addition, the tests monitor acoustics, fuel efficiency, and emissions, to better protect air quality and the environment.

The section through the GE property has not been blazed for years, and I make a note to the BTA. A hiker must navigate through this property because there are no roads which parallel the area. Any alternative would require a very, very long road walk.

I pull out the BT map, note the topographic features of the land, and read the description for this area. After perhaps half a mile, we do find a faded blaze that appears to have been painted during the construction of the trail 40 years ago. Following the map directions, we continue and find, over the two-mile stretch, no more than four very faint and highly weathered blazes. With map and blazes, we are able to successfully pass through the GE property.

Then we have 1.6 miles on roads before we come to our next off-road section, a trail which runs for two miles through the Davis Memorial State Nature Preserve.

At the entrance to Davis Memorial, we are leave the Sinking Spring Section of the BT and entering the Shawnee Section.

The nature preserve's 88-acre wood prairie is beautiful. It has been a while since we have been on an off-road section that has a good trail and beautiful scenery. There are also plaques along the trail providing information about plants, the dolomite rock outcrops, and the stream that flows through the preserve. One plaque describes a fault line that has shifted the rocks. A good geologist could point out the difference between one side of the fault and the other, but I cannot. The trail also goes by a menacing sinkhole about 12 feet in diameter; the dark abyss goes down further than I can see!

Davis Memorial State Nature Preserve

We exit the preserve and enter a pasture with cattle that move off at our approach. From the next field, we can see our destination for tonight—Mineral Springs Lake Resort, still a couple of miles away.

This 580-acre resort in the Appalachian foothills was created by Billy Lee Smalley. The campground encompasses 80 acres, with 300 campsites. "Resort" gives this place a grand-sounding name, but it is really another RV and trailer park in a country setting. We, however, are allowed to primitive camp anywhere we choose, and we find a site overlooking the lake and near the beach.

The land around the lake has, for the most part, been left beautifully wooded.

The lake, at 103 acres, is one of the largest privately owned lakes in Ohio. Gas-engine boats are forbidden on the lake; this helps to keep the water pristine. The very clean water supports bass, bluegill, and an unusual freshwater jellyfish. The freshwater jellyfish is quite small, only one inch in diameter, and feeds on microscopic zooplankton. Originally native to China, the jellyfish probably were transported to the States with ornamental aquatic plants. They are now found in shallow, slow-moving bodies of water in parts of the Midwest and the Great Lakes area.

We use the showers and hang out in the shade of the neighboring picnic shelter while we write notes, read, and eat snacks, ice cream, and V8 juice from the camp store.

After a long hike, sleep comes easily on our lakeside perch.

Mineral Springs Lake Resort

TICKS AND SOUTHERN OHIO

Day 40: May 31, Tuesday

We have a different alarm clock this morning. There are enough Canada geese on the lake to create a racket at daybreak, and there is no sleeping within a thin-walled tent.

We do not begrudge the geese for waking us, though, when we see that our campsite gives us a glorious view of the sunrise over the lake. Clouds hang in the eastern sky, but enough light comes through to create splendid colors.

We head out of camp at 6:20 a.m. and are on the Buckeye Trail at 6:50. It is 60 degrees—pleasantly cool for a morning walk. The hike out of the resort is much quieter than the entry yesterday, when so many vehicles were coming or going.

We're in a new section of the Buckeye Trail—the Shawnee Section—and the neighborhood we hike through this morning is real friendly. A large dog charges down a lawn as we approach, gives us a sniff, barks a good morning, and lets us pass. A bullfrog croaks a morning greeting, and then turkeys gobble a pleasant good morning.

Hiking on, we pass a historic marker that tells us about the resort that once existed here—a grand hotel, businesses, and recreational venues, where vacationers took advantage of the peaceful surroundings and the medicinal properties of the springs at the foot of Peach Mountain. The main hotel burned down in 1924 and was never rebuilt, and the rest of the buildings were left to succumb to weather and disrepair. All that remains are stone structures around the springs.

Today's hike will be 100 percent road walk, which means we can hike the 21.7 miles in about eight hours. By 9:30 a.m., it is 70 degrees in the shade; by 10:00, the temperature in the sun is 90 degrees. Our umbrellas provide refreshing shade, and it is delightful to be able to hike without our skulls being cooked by the sun. We continue to find ways to attach the handles of our silver domes to our shoulder and chest straps so that our hands are free.

A road bridge crosses over Rocky Fork stream, aptly named because the clear, cool water is tumbling over bedrock. We follow the

WANDERING OHIO

Road Walk

stream for a couple of miles. The Buckeye Trail then turns onto Big Spruce-Little Bear Creek Road. At the junction, a sign states: *Road will be closed May 31 – June 1.*

Today, of course, is May 31.

However, we have no choice; our destination, Ben's Happy Trails Stables and Horseman's Camp, is 3.5 miles down that road. We venture forth, in spite of the sign.

When we finally arrive at the construction, the road crew is installing a culvert across the road right at the horse camp. The backhoe operator sees us, smiles, and pauses to let us pass.

The horse camp has a very friendly atmosphere. A sign in the lodge's common area brings a humble tear to my eye with its welcome: *There is always room around here for one more jackass!*

Shaun, the foreman, greets us and explains that lodging options include one of three self-contained cabins for $75, camping for $15, and lodge rooms for $40 (provide your own bedding). We have our own bedding, so we choose the lodge room for the convenience of showers, sitting areas, and work space.

First, we wash off the day's sweat in the lodge's common shower room; then we set off to explore the grounds. We look into a cabin—very adequate, with kitchen, AC, shower, and bedroom. We check out the horse barn, rabbit cages, chicken coop (with a pair of peacocks), and some geese around the farm pond. The camp owns 27 horses and boards another 13.

Ben's Horseman's Camp

Ben acquired the 100 acres 30 years ago when he was in his early forties. He was living in Dayton but spent many days riding a horse around Shawnee State Forest. Originally from Tennessee, he was reminded of home by the hills in Shawnee State Forest—they're called the "Little Smokies." We are hoping the feel of the famous Great

Smoky Mountains will embrace us as we hike into Shawnee State Forest tomorrow.

At supper time, a couple of individuals are driving to town to pick up pizzas. Beth acts quickly and puts in an order for a medium cheese pizza. What comes back looks more like a large pizza. We eat two-thirds of it and save the rest for tomorrow's brunch.

Day 41: June 1, Wednesday

A rooster begins crowing quite early, but at 5 a.m., a whippoorwill has to show the rooster how it is really done and sings out several 100-plus repetitions of its distinctive "whip-poor-will" calls. At the end, a donkey gets its two cents in with a couple of loud brays.

Thus awakened, we set off down the road toward Shawnee State Forest at 6:10, with a waning crescent moon in the eastern sky and stars fading in the morning light.

After a couple of miles, the road increases in elevation; and through an opening in the trees, we catch a glimpse of a valley filled with a light fog. Our first taste of the Little Smokies!

Forest Road – Shawnee State Park

TICKS AND SOUTHERN OHIO

We proceed onto a bridle trail which is, fortunately, in good condition. The trail is easy to hike, even with its ups and downs, but the trees block views of the surrounding area. Emerging onto State Route 125, we walk to the lodge entrance road where Beth flags down a pickup truck and we are quickly driven up to the lodge, saving us a 1.5-mile hike off the Buckeye Trail. It is only 9 a.m., but the lodge desk attendant lets us check into a room early. We hastily unpack, shower, and settle in for a relaxing day. This qualifies as a nero day, a short hiking day on the trail.

We are in a state forest created from the former hunting grounds of the Shawnee Indians. They had established a town, Lower Town, near both the Ohio and the Scioto Rivers, and they used these rivers to travel across central and southern Ohio. The Shawnee name means "those who have silver." Apparently, they were known to do business using this metal.

The rivers were also a major waterway for the pioneers pushing westward, settlers who were determined to clear the forest and build cabins and towns. During the 1700s, many confrontations between settlers and natives gradually displaced the Shawnee nation.

In the 1920s, the state of Ohio created a game preserve in this area. The next decade saw the building of roads and lakes; and in 1949, Shawnee State Forest and Shawnee State Park were formed from 63,000 acres in the foothills of the Appalachians. This is now the largest of Ohio's 18 state forests.

Shawnee Lodge has 50 rooms, and there are 25 cabins in the park as well. We eat a late lunch at the lodge restaurant—I have a salad and chili and Beth has a hummus wrap with sweet potato fries—and afterward, we migrate to the pool for an hour and a half, where we also visit the snack stand and indulge in an ice cream sandwich.

Three hundred years ago, what might have been happening on this very spot?

We're happy to be here. It is a hot day, near 90 degrees, and a perfect day to be at a pool—and eating ice cream!

We are clean, our gear is reorganized, and we have time to look around the lodge, make phone calls and, of course, work on BT section notes and our journal.

We have dinner at the lodge at 6:30 p.m. and order two delicious meals of salmon, baked potato, and broccoli. This is also a celebratory meal—we are now at the halfway point of our BT hike around Ohio! Tomorrow will mark six weeks since our start at Headlands Beach.

Day 42: June 2, Thursday

This morning, I'm up at 6:00 to hike a section of the Buckeye Trail and then return to the lodge via a service road.

The hike has a two-fold purpose. I want to hike and review the BT near to and away from the lodge, for one thing. The other reason for my early-morning walk is that if I complete this section, Beth and I may use the service road (a faster route) to rejoin the Buckeye Trail tomorrow, giving us a head start on the day.

I find that the BT within the park is well marked, but with orange blazes instead of blue. The park service has done an excellent job of maintaining the trail, and I make good progress along the trail by jog-walking. In my rush, I may have caught a turkey sleeping. Whatever the case, we startle each other as it flies up from its resting place not 15 feet from me.

Though the forecast did not call for rain, it rains during my hike—of course. I am already sweating, and the rain only makes me a little wetter, but I am still comfortable. When the trail intersects the service road, I return to the lodge and happily take a shower before Beth and I head to the restaurant for a late breakfast.

Beth does laundry while I write notes for the databook. When our laundry is done, we head back to the restaurant for an afternoon lunch. We order a light meal and also hummus wraps for the trail tomorrow. We have managed to fill every crevice in our stomachs, and we will forgo dinner.

We relax in the room and snack before retiring for the day.

TICKS AND SOUTHERN OHIO

Day 43: June 3, Friday

Once again, it is during the night that a thunderstorm passes, from 9 to 10 p.m.—while we are comfy in a bed.

We are up at 5 a.m., eat four hardboiled eggs that we obtained from the restaurant yesterday, and check out at 5:35. The early morning is warm, with a mist among the trees. The portion of the sky we see through the tree canopy is baby blue with white puffy clouds.

As we cross Deadman Hollow Road, a forest worker approaches in a pickup truck with a large water tank in the back. He explains that the forest service fills the water tank near the trail for people to obtain drinking water.

We see a turtle and a toad, and pass a small country Church of God that is still in use. If you attend services there and have to use the restroom, you will be obliged to use the pit toilets out back. Actually, most churches we pass in this area use privies rather than flush toilets because the area is so remote.

We rest on a bench overlooking the church's cemetery and eat half our hummus sandwich from the restaurant.

Road Walk

For 7.8 miles, we hike along Sunshine Ridge Road, a very deserted gravel byway. It seems so isolated as to feel lonely—there is no breeze, only a few birds chirp, and we are closed in by the trees. Small family cemeteries are numerous through southern Ohio and the trail goes by several of them.

Signs along the roads give the resident family's name. Toward the end of our day's hike, we descend an unmaintained dirt road before it meets a short, maintained stretch and then turns to pavement. Along this section, we find the name on a mailbox we were hoping to find—*Don Fiedler.* He has allowed hikers to spend the night on his property for years.

No one is home, so we pull out a couple of lawn chairs that are leaning against a work shed, and we sit in the shade of a tree to eat the remainder of the hummus wrap, relax, and wait.

It is not long before a neighbor drives up—Troy, accompanied by his son Dodge. They tell us that Don passed away this winter at 85 years of age. Troy now watches the Fiedler place while Don's wife, Peggy, is in Dayton with her daughter. Troy calls Peggy to let her know we are here and then opens a simple hunter's cabin that Don built years ago.

Beth brooms out the dust and cobwebs, and we settle in. Once again, by moving early we have completed a 20-mile hike by early afternoon, with the reward of sitting in the shade, eating snacks, and writing during the heat of the day.

Two biting deerflies appear on the scene for us to deal with. Thankfully, we have now hiked through nearly all the southern off-road sections and have suffered only a few minor rashes of poison ivy.

The cicadas' low hum can be heard as we fall asleep.

Day 44: June 4, Saturday

Rising at 5:25 a.m., we need a flashlight to pack. Outside the rustic cabin, the sky is overcast and gray and the air is humid. We are on the Buckeye Trail by 5:55. Again there is only a slight breeze, and everything is unusually quiet except for a few cicadas.

TICKS AND SOUTHERN OHIO

We start off on a paved road and pass homes with lots of junk cars or just general junk—which seems to be a basic theme in southern Ohio. Many places also have dogs penned up, and these people may not love our early morning hiking schedule because the dogs bark incessantly as we pass.

Yesterday we finished the Shawnee Section of the BT, and today we are hiking in the West Union Section.

Abner Hollow is a gravel road 1.5 miles long with no homes, a short uphill, and then a descent along a deep, rocky ravine that plunges to a stream flowing over bedrock in a series of miniature cascades and waterfalls.

The road spills out into the Ohio Brush Creek valley where a mist hangs halfway up the hillsides. The May rains have given the fields and forests a lush appearance and filled the streams with plenty of water. We cross over Brush Creek on a relatively new bridge.

Along this road, we come to a home that has long, curving stone walls. The owner is standing on the porch, perhaps 200 feet away from us. We call out, "Good morning!"

He is hard of hearing and walks toward the road to meet us. When we compliment him on the walls, he tells us he built them himself. I spot a fossilized horn coral lying on one of the limestone pieces.

"Come with me. I'll show you some fossils," he offers.

As we walk toward the porch, Beth asks if he has found any arrowheads. His answer is a definite *yes*, but he adds dejectedly that his very large arrowhead collection was stolen.

Across the top of his porch railing, he has built a wooden tray and filled it with dozens of fossils. We examine and admire them.

As we all walk back toward the road, he tells me that the motto people should live by is that "Everybody's got something." I am sure he was referring to more than material possessions.

As we turn onto State Route 247 at 9:45 a.m., it starts to rain. Our umbrellas go up for about an hour as the light shower passes.

We turn left onto Bat Roost Road, and Beth notes a church about 300 feet to the right. I walk up to investigate and find that the church has a picnic shelter, tables, a privy, and even an outside water hydrant—everything a hiker would need, especially the water. I make a note of it for the databook.

The Ohio River is only one or two miles away, and Bat Roost Road offers some beautiful views in the river's direction, although the river is just out of view. The Kentucky hills loom in the distance. As we watch goldfinches, cardinals, and woodpeckers, Beth speculates that road walks allow us to see a larger variety of birds. Footpaths generally lead through the woods, whereas road walks offer a variety of bird habitats as the roads go through woods, fields, and suburbs.

At 1:15 p.m., we arrive in Bentonville (population 327), where we find a monument to the Bentonville Anti-Horse Thief Society, an organization that has been in continuous existence since 1853. Members formed a posse, retrieved stolen horses, and hung horse thieves. Goodness knows what they do today, though I hear the Society still functions as a social club.

Burning Heart Campground is 0.6 mile south of the trail, on State Route 41. I learned of its existence from Google Maps but could not determine its operational status. We hike to the campground, and it does not appear to have been used for a number of years. I knock on the doors of neighbors to inquire about the campground but cannot find anyone who can provide a contact phone number.

We put Plan B into action and hitchhike north to the Country Inn, located on the south side of West Union. This turns out to be a good plan—a thunderstorm and pouring rain descend on us from 4 to 5 p.m. and again around 8 p.m., but we are already at the inn.

Between the storms, we walk a couple of blocks to Frisch's Big Boy restaurant and enjoy an excellent fish sandwich and the soup, salad, and fruit bar. With our appetites satiated, we return to our room to relax and write in the journal as the second storm passes.

It has been so long since we found any money that we were almost ready to eat our shoe-sole inserts for lack of funds. But we had a banner day and found $0.60. Our hike marches on!

TICKS AND SOUTHERN OHIO

Day 45: June 5, Sunday

This morning, our internal alarms, adjusted for hiking, wake us at 5:30. However, Frisch's Big Boy does not open until 7 a.m., and we are not about to pass up a good breakfast, so today's start is delayed.

After breakfast, we hoist our packs and step out the motel door, walk a few steps down the road, and—Beth looks at the sky.

"Don't those clouds look like rain?" she remarks.

I concur, pull out my phone, check the radar, and sure enough, another major storm is coming within a few minutes.

We hasten back to the motel, grab our room key from the drop box, and wait out the storm over the next hour.

Once the rain is past, we hitch a ride back to the trail fairly quickly. At the restaurant this morning, we overheard that the area has received four inches of rain over the past week. As testimony to that statement, the ditches and culverts are flowing full. Streams run muddier as they wash soil from the plowed fields. We do not want to be fording any streams after the storms of yesterday and this morning.

We notice that the land is flatter, barely rolling, and grain fields are replacing cattle farms. It is obvious that we are gradually hiking out of the hills of Appalachia and into the glaciated portion of Ohio.

Before glaciation, Ohio was much different than the state we know today. Lake Erie did not exist; instead, a major river (Erigans River) flowed in a wide valley where the lake is today.

About two million years ago, the warm climate of the Cenozoic era cooled sufficiently for snow and ice to begin to accumulate in the far northern latitudes. As the ice thickness increased, it slowly flowed outward and into the northern United States. At least four major periods of glaciation occurred, with numerous retreats and advances in the ice during those periods. The last glacier entered Ohio about 24,000 years ago, and retreated out of Ohio about 14,000 years ago. At its furthest extent, the mile-thick ice covered two-thirds of the state.

Glacial grooves on Kelley's Island in Lake Erie are among the most famous of Ohio's glacially eroded features. Most of the hills that we will encounter in the coming days and weeks will be moraines, glacier-created mounds of pulverized bedrock and soil that are up to 100 feet high and several miles wide. Glacial deposits are now mined for sand and gravel, and they contain large boulders or rocks that are not native to Ohio but were carried down in the ice from Canada.

By 11 a.m., the clouds begin to disperse, and where the pavement is not shaded, the sun quickly dries the road. Just as we turn onto Martin Hollow Road, a pickup truck pulls up and the driver inquires, "Are you hiking the Buckeye Trail?" A rare phrase—we are still not used to hearing this!

The driver's name is Mike Vogel. He is on his way to Shawnee State Park for a day hike. The Buckeye Trail goes past his property, which we will see tomorrow.

In the middle of the afternoon, we catch a ride into Georgetown, to the Bailey House Bed and Breakfast. The house was originally built by Dr. Bailey in 1830. It was then sold to the Thompson family, who has retained ownership for at least three generations.

Georgetown is also the boyhood home of Ulysses S. Grant. (Ulysses was born elsewhere, but his family moved to Georgetown when he was one year old.) The following is from a display outside the Grant home:

> Grant's father, Jesse, built the family home and a tannery across the street.
>
> Work in a tannery was bloody and smelly—livestock were slaughtered, their hides soaked in lye and then cured with acid. When Grant was not at school, he was expected to contribute by working at the tannery in the bark mill grinding bark or in the beam shop cleaning hides of flesh, hair, and dirt.
>
> Grant disliked the tannery and preferred to work with horses. At age 7 he could drive a team of horses and began to haul wood used in the house and tannery. At age 11 he plowed the fields, brought in the crops, and

took over "all the work done with horses," as he recalled in his memoirs. By age 14 Grant owned and operated a livery service, in which he, as the sole driver, delivered passengers all over Ohio.

In 1840, after Grant went to the military academy at West Point, Jesse and Hannah Grant and their remaining children moved to Bethel, Ohio. Ulysses Grant never again lived in the Georgetown house.

The Grant family home is only a block from the Bailey House B&B, and during Grant's childhood, the two families were not only neighbors but also friends. At the age of 17, Grant received an appointment from West Point to fill a vacancy created when the Baileys' son, Bart, left West Point to attend a private school. Ulysses first declared he would not go; he wrote in his memoirs that he did not believe he had the "acquirements necessary to get through" and was afraid of failing and causing his family and his town embarrassment. His father encouraged him, though, and he not only graduated but also became such a brave and effective military leader that President Lincoln claimed "I can't spare this man!"

At the Grant home, we pay for a 30-minute tour. The first part of the brick house was built in 1823, the kitchen was added in 1825, another section was added in 1827, and the final portion added in 1828. The brick home was well built and comfortable for that time in history, though it is not nearly as grand as the Bailey House.

We also cross paths again with Brigadier General John Hunt Morgan. In search of food and supplies, the general's brother, Colonel Richard Morgan, led about 200 of their men into Georgetown on the morning of July 15, 1863. A plaque in front of the courthouse describes the events and quotes a letter Elizabeth King wrote to Ulysses S. Grant in 1884, to tell him about the raid.

> The raiders' systematic search of stables and sheds produced only a single horse, owned by William

Ellsberry. Other raiders focused on plundering dry goods and shoe stores, "taking the best, carrying off many pieces of silk and all they could possibly carry away." A search of the former Grant home on East Grant Avenue proved fruitless. When the raiders broke into the post office, they found two muskets. "They broke them over the rocks and left them in the street."

Some raiders went to each house asking for food. "The ladies gave them all they asked for," King reported. "They were all very polite and bowing and lifting their hats when leaving." Colonel Morgan asked Mrs. John Stuart for "a piece of bread and butter with a glass of buttermilk" but was interrupted by an orderly when half finished. The Colonel got up in a hurry and "the bugle sounded and in less than five minutes they were all mounted and left town."

    The owner of the Bailey house, Nancy, and one of her friends drive us to the Country Inn restaurant and join us for dinner. During the evening's conversation, Beth and I learn that we are staying in the room once used by Steve Newman, famously known as "The Worldwalker," while he was writing his book about his walk around the world.

    After dinner, Nancy drives to the one-room school house where Grant received his early education. The school was designed by an architect who then became the school's teacher for 23 years.

    We make one last stop at the United Dairy Store to purchase supplies for a couple of days before retiring to our room.

Bailey House Bed and Breakfast

Day 46: June 6, Monday

Nancy cooks up an appetizing breakfast of eggs, biscuits, and fresh fruit. She talks about another hiker she assisted, providing transportation to and from the trail. The thought occurs to me that since we are essentially doing a radius hike around Georgetown, Nancy could pick us up and return us to her B&B for the night. She willingly consents. So Beth and I anticipate a lovely slackpack day.

By 8 a.m., we are on the trail—without the burden of backpacks, thanks to our trail angel.

The evening storms have ushered in a beautiful, bright morning, and the drier air holds a faint, refreshing scent of honeysuckle. As we hike down a road with trees on either side, Beth comments on the rich blue of the sky we glimpse between the treetops. Just as I look up, an eagle flies over the opening in the canopy, and in the morning sun, its white head gleams against the azure sky.

We soon arrive at the wooded area owned by Mike Vogel, the man we met yesterday. Camping is permitted there, and we explore the area before hiking a couple tenths of a mile to his home, which is visible from the wooded site.

Mike must have been watching our activities; as we approach his farm lane, he drives out on an ATV to greet us. We talk about his hike yesterday at Shawnee State Park and his plans for another section hike on the Appalachian Trail this year. He is anxious to get on the trail, waiting only until the fields are dry enough for him to get his hay cut and baled—and then he'll be off to the trail.

Today we will hike into the Williamsburg Section, and Mike thinks he has heard something about a portion of it being closed. He uses his smart phone and pulls up the Buckeye Trail website, then reads to us what he has found—the off-road section along the south side of Harsha Lake in East Fork State Park has been bulldozed and is therefore closed. This involves nearly 26 miles of trail, and the reroute eliminates 18 miles of the Williamsburg section. Mike is our second trail angel for today. I'm generally so busy making notes for the databook that I may not have caught that trail announcement.

With that news to contemplate, we continue with our hike. The landscape around Georgetown is perhaps 50 percent wood lots and 50 percent farmland, a pleasant combination to view as we walk.

The BT turns onto a road that is nearly abandoned and it dead-ends at an overhead bridge that crosses a river to our left. Approaching the bridge, we are astonished to see a fox dart out from the brush, run down to the end of the road, and disappear again in the brush. A rare and exciting sight for us!

The path under the bridge is overgrown and quite impassible. We backtrack and use the overhead bridge to cross over the brush-choked trail. The small delay and detour are serendipitous—to rejoin the BT, we walk through a covered bridge!

We are using our umbrellas for shade, but by early afternoon it becomes too windy, so the umbrellas are put away and the wind will have to keep us cool.

The trail takes us past Grant Lake, on the south side of Mount Orab. My expectation of this lake was that we would find a shoreline with areas for picnicking and relaxation. However, as we cross over the dam and look up at the lake, we see no activity except a couple of fishermen near the dam. The shore appears to be completely forested.

Although the trail is on the road following the west side of the lake, we do not even see the water. At a boat launch, we can walk to the water's edge, but we find no resting place for weary hikers along Grant Lake.

When we reach our day's destination, we give Nancy a call. Within half an hour, we are riding back for a second pleasant night at the bed and breakfast. A 20-plus-mile hike exhausts us, but today, at least, we did not have to carry our backpacks, and we greatly appreciated that.

In the evening, I spend some time reviewing the Williamsburg Section, researching the trail that is closed around East Fork State Park Harsha Lake. Apparently, changes are being made to accommodate horseback riders and the trail has been bulldozed—but now it has deteriorated into a muddy mess, not suitable for foot travel.

As we look back over our walk to date, we agree that the disruption of the trail by logging and the tick infestation added stress to our hike and made the days we spent in the Scioto Trail Section the most difficult time, mentally, that we have experienced thus far on the Buckeye Trail.

Chapter 7

SOUTHERN TERMINUS

Day 47: June 7, Tuesday
At breakfast, we meet two gentlemen who also stayed at the B&B last night. Both are originally from Detroit; one moved to Alabama, and the other now resides in Georgetown. Occasionally they get together and travel to areas of mutual interest, and today they're headed to Cincinnati. When they offer us a ride back to the Buckeye Trail, we accept.

The day is perfect, with low humidity and a high temperature expected in the 70s.

Unexpectedly, we find a box turtle along the road. Will it be the last one we see as we now head into the farmland and more urban areas of western Ohio?

We stop at a gas station food mart in the town of Batavia and make a phone call to arrange for a shuttle to the southern terminus of the BT in Cincinnati at Eden Park. The BT from the Williamsburg Section joins the Loveland Section 13 miles north of what was the southern terminus before the trail became a loop. We wish to see this point in Eden Park, so we must either walk the 13 miles down and 13 miles back, or else make shuttle arrangements. Beth also makes a call to her cousin, Laura, who lives in the Cincinnati area.

As we head toward an urban area, our expectation at every bend is to see lots of houses, but even five miles away from Milford (population 6,683), the landscape is still farmland, woods, rivers, and even a log building on a lake. In the background, we now hear the rush of traffic on Interstate 275, a sound we have not heard for a long time.

Turning onto Round Bottom Road, we encounter traffic—a little too close for comfort. Cars go zipping by, and there is virtually no berm. The sounds of flowing water and chirping birds can only be heard during brief traffic interludes. We have now gone from a landscape where homes were surrounded by hundreds of acres to one of apartment buildings and houses with yards that barely have room to plant peonies. Large vegetable gardens are now rare sights, as rare as passing greetings and questions about our walk. Not even a bicyclist acknowledges us on Round Bottom Road. We walk under I-275, and the superhighway flows over us. The last such highway we passed under was I-77, several weeks ago.

Not everyone is insensitive to our passing, though. We have had three offers of water since leaving Batavia, and, given the increasingly impersonal, rushing atmosphere, this is amazing to us—and almost unbelievable.

We stroll into Milford through a neighborhood of well-tended, quaint old homes. Many have beautiful landscaping and ornate porch columns painted in multi-colors and harkening back to a time when people sat outside on hot summer days and watched the world go by.

Downtown, we find a vibrant historic area, and we seek out the Roads Rivers and Trails (RRT) outdoor equipment store. The owner, Brian, graciously assists hikers and has volunteered to shuttle us to the southern terminus of the BT. We meet a couple of the staff at RRT, but Brian has left for the day. We will have to wait to meet him until tomorrow morning, at the designated shuttle time.

We go across the street to Padrino, an Italian restaurant, where I order lasagna and Beth has a Caesar salad. A few tables sit out on the sidewalk, and the temperature is perfect for dining *al fresco*. Conveniently located next door is an ice cream store, so the dessert decision has been made for us.

We are waiting for Beth's cousin Laura to meet us. We will spend the next two nights at her condo in Sharonville, northeast of Cincinnati. When she arrives, our trail angel also excitedly tells us that she has arranged for a day off from work tomorrow and can join us for the 13-mile walk from the southern terminus to Milford.

At Laura's condo, we shower and I catch up on journal notes while Beth and her cousin catch up on family news.

Day 48: June 8, Wednesday

This is our fourth "late-start" morning, but we still wake up with the birds. Laura has oatmeal on the breakfast menu, a dish we have not had for quite some time. We indulge in this culinary delight, mixing in brown sugar, raisins, and walnuts.

After breakfast, we return to Milford and meet Brian at his RRT store. Brian is a hiker himself, so we enjoy a pleasurable conversation about hiking adventures and the BT, and our travel time to the southern terminus in Eden Park passes quickly. This engaging conversation makes us realize how much we have missed the interaction with other hikers that we've had on our previous hikes.

The southern terminus at Eden Park is on a high bluff overlooking the Ohio River. The spot offers a marvelous view of the Ohio River and Kentucky, on the river's southern bank.

A 30-foot obelisk of granite stands here, dedicated by President Herbert Hoover in 1929 to commemorate the canalization of the Ohio River. The obelisk really has nothing to do with the BT; the overlook, however, provides a grand view for the southern terminus of a trail that celebrates the state of Ohio.

Eden Park encompasses 186 acres that were purchased by the city in 1869 from Nicholas Longworth, a prominent Cincinnati landowner and horticulturalist who had used the land as a vineyard. It is now home to the Cincinnati Art Museum, Cincinnati Playhouse in the Park, and the Krohn Conservatory, and it is one of the most popular of Cincinnati's parks.

The original Buckeye Trail went only from the northern terminus on Lake Erie (where we started) to this southern point. That trail was completed in October 1970, and only later was the BT extended to form the big loop around Ohio (completed in 1980). We have hiked through eastern and southern Ohio, approximately 830 miles of the loop, and will now be heading up the western side of Ohio.

At the Obelisk in Eden Park

We spend some time doing photo shoots at the obelisk before meandering through the park. Quickly picking up the trail, we come across a wooden sign at a less conspicuous location with the carved words

BUCKEYE TRAIL
SOUTHERN TERMINUS
FOLLOW THE BLUE BLAZES

The day promises to be a carbon copy of yesterday, with cool temperatures and a sky full of puffy, white cumulus clouds. Our walk will be on sidewalks and bike paths, but Laura has not hiked 13 miles before, so it will be a new experience for her.

At 0.7 mile, we find a conflict between the blue blazes and the BT map instructions. We follow the blue blazes; however, I believe the map (and databook being developed) show the correct route. The difference is only a few city blocks, but the conflict will need to be resolved within the BTA.

The first 9.2 miles are on city sidewalks. We pass city parks and find a drinking fountain conveniently located on a corner along the trail. Only five miles into our hike, we pass a Graeter's ice cream store, and Laura informs us it is the world's best ice cream. I'm certain there is an unwritten law that states a hiker is not permitted to pass up an ice cream establishment; and being law-abiding hikers, we are taking no chances. We order a pint of raspberry chocolate chip ice cream and split it between the three of us.

Proceeding down the street while enjoying our ice cream, we pass several restaurants, food marts, and even a Kroger grocery store. We have seen more food in the first nine miles then we've seen in the last few weeks.

The blue blazes join a bike/hike trail, and we find a plaque with history about the trail that we are now about to traverse. It follows what was once the corridor for the area's first railroad. In 1836, the Little Miami Railroad was chartered and started running from Cincinnati to Milford in 1841. The trip took up to four hours to complete, mostly due to numerous stops and because the structure of the track only allowed for slow speeds. The original track was a wooden structure covered with strips of iron. Since the locomotive was fueled with wood, there was a constant danger of fires being ignited by sparks. Trains entering Cincinnati stopped east of the city and were pulled in by horses and mules to avoid any fires occurring downtown. The line was eventually sold to the Pennsylvania Railroad, and they abandoned it in 1974.

As we approach Milford and the end of our day's hike, I make contact with a person we know as "Apple." Beth and I first met him two years ago while hiking the Colorado Trail. We were coming down a long, hot stretch of trail in July 2014, and saw a person waiting underneath a large pine tree in the distance. A horse trailer was also part of the scene, and we assumed this was somebody waiting for a group on horseback. As we approached him, he greeted us and told us he was there to assist hikers. He had been expecting us, he said.

Expecting us? How could he possibly have been expecting us?

Apple told us he had buried a ground sensor on the trail—and it pinged his phone whenever a hiker passed over it!

The area was remote and nearly barren, but this trail angel had constructed a temporary geodesic dome covered with tarps, and inside he placed drinks, snacks, and—most importantly—good, fresh water. This was all a very welcome sight at that point in our hike. The section of the Colorado trail we had just gone through lacked water, and the streams that existed were fouled with farm runoff.

We learned that Apple was from Cincinnati, so we hoped to meet him again. We were fortunately able to do that later in 2014, over dinner in Logan.

When I phone him now, Apple agrees to drive down from his West Chester home and meet us in Milford. We arrive in Milford at 3:30 p.m. and stop at the Roads Rivers and Trails store to once again thank Brian for driving us to the southern terminus and tell him we had a wonderful hike back to Milford.

Laura hiked very well and added much to our hike with her knowledge of Cincinnati and the sites we saw along the way. While Beth is purchasing a lightweight, insect-repellent shirt at Brian's store, Apple meets us there.

Laura recommends a restaurant along the bikeway, a short drive up in nearby Loveland.

At the Trailside Café, over sandwiches and wraps, we catch up on news from Apple. In the first half of this year, he has already provided trail magic for hikers on the Appalachian Trail and the Colorado Trail, and he intends to go back to the Colorado Trail later this summer. He also enjoys bicycling and has recently completed rides from his home to Columbus and from his home to Chillicothe. Last year he rode to Cleveland on the cross-state bike trail.

The weather was fantastic for our walk and outdoor café dining, and the company and conversation were fascinating, making this a memorable day.

SOUTHERN TERMINUS

Day 49: June 9, Thursday

We wake up at 5 a.m. and spend an hour packing and preparing to resume our hike with full backpacks. We eat more oatmeal, and Laura kindly drives us to Milford, where we will pick up the trail heading north toward Loveland and Kings Mills.

At 7:30 a.m., we say goodbye to our trail angel and step onto the bike-hike trail. A rabbit nibbles grass along the edge of the path, hops down the trail, and darts into the bushes as we approach. About that time, a squirrel scampers across the trail. The number of bicyclists gradually increases, but it's a weekday, and they are not numerous enough for us to be bothered by their presence. The phrase "on your left" is, however, repeated often as the bikers swish by.

General Morgan first began stirring up trouble in Ohio near this area. We are close to the point where he entered Ohio from Indiana and continued his march across the southern part of the state. This will probably be the last time our hike crosses the General's path, since his campaign headed east and we are now heading north.

It was Tuesday morning, July 14, 1863, that the Union officer Lieutenant Colonel George Neff was informed of General Morgan's approach with more than 2,000 Confederate cavalrymen. The Union troops had been warned two days earlier that Morgan would attack, and they had dug in for a fight. Morgan's veteran soldiers dismounted and began a brisk firefight. The Confederate troops used two howitzers to shell the Union position for nearly 30 minutes before retreating to Montgomery.

Morgan's Raiders, as history has dubbed them, were not to be deterred. They derailed a passenger train pulled by the locomotive *Kilgore* and stumbled upon the deserted Camp Shady, a Union supply depot. Much to the raiders' delight, they found 50 U.S. Army covered wagons that had been left behind, as well as a drove of horses and mules. General Morgan ordered the wagons to be searched for needed items and then burned. The raiders continued their march southeast toward Batavia, Williamsburg, and Georgetown, where we last crossed his trail a couple of days ago.

In an hour, we cross a bridge over the Little Miami River. I snap a picture, and memory takes me back 40 years to a day when I raced a kayak down this river in the National Marathon Canoe and Kayak races. Today there are pleasure canoeists on the river, enjoying the beautiful day. Some boaters float along singing, while others splash in the water.

Bike Path (near Loveland)

Around 10:30 a.m., we arrive in Loveland (population 12,326), where we had dinner last night. This time we choose Julian's Deli, another restaurant on the bike trail, for a late morning breakfast. Beth has scrambled eggs on a croissant, and I have an egg salad sandwich. We relax and enjoy the morning for almost an hour before we head north again.

A little after noon, we pass a couple with two kids who are out for a bike ride. They have stopped to rest on a trailside bench, and as we walk by, I hear the word *labas*.

I take a few steps and look quizzically at Beth, and she is looking at me in surprise.

Beth spent 20 years in Lithuania before we met, and I have learned to recognize a couple of Lithuanian words. If we heard correctly, we have just been given a *Good morning* in Lithuanian. I look back over my shoulder.

"Labas," I say, and their faces light up. Beth's face lights up, too.

We turn around and go back to them, and Beth begins a conversation in Lithuanian. She finds out they moved to the United States 18 years ago. There is a Lithuanian community in the Cincinnati area, and the couple invites us to join them at one of their festivities someday. We exchange phone numbers and hope that we will meet them again at a Lithuanian festivity in Cincinnati.

The trail passes within a couple of miles of Kings Mills, where Kings Island Amusement Resort is located. We can hear the screams of people enjoying the more thrilling rides.

The bike path is paved and lined by trees that generally provide shade over the trail. By 1 p.m., the sun is high enough to penetrate the canopy, and we raise our umbrellas to make our own shade.

By 4:30 p.m., we are in the small crossroad town of Morrow (population 1,229) and seek out the Sugar Run Grill for dinner. Our hike today was 22.5 miles, and we would like to spend more time relaxing as we enjoy our dinner; but when I make a phone call to the nearby Little Miami Canoe Rental and Campground, I find they are going to close by 6 p.m. We hustle over and pay the camping fee and get a tour of the campsites. We are tired, and we choose to be near the restroom/shower building of the canoe business area. It's only for the night, and we will be up early and on our way.

A high school student keeps a red-tailed hawk near the office building and uses the bird for hunting. Beth watches him handle the hawk and learns about falconry while I finish the day, working on our notes and journal.

Day 50: June 10, Friday

I slept really well last night; Beth, a bit more fitfully. We both dutifully begin to pack up at 6:05 a.m. At 6:50, we are on the trail, with the temperature in the upper 50s.

It is early on a Friday morning, and the trail is ours until we meet two retired teachers, out for a morning walk along the tree-lined bikeway. After a short chat with them, we walk on, passing farm fields. A deer bounds through one field, and a short time later, two turkeys run from an open area into the woods. A woodpecker is somewhere, making itself heard. A deerfly bites my neck, and I swat a couple of mosquitoes. Is this a sampling of things to come? I have wondered that at other times on this hike, but so far, mosquitoes and deerflies have not been too much of a problem.

The northwest horizon looks ominously dark. The chance of rain today was forecasted to be zero percent. I pull out my phone (isn't technology marvelous?) and check the radar. A large mass of green, yellow, and even red blotches are headed our way. The rain will begin at 8:15 a.m., says the forecast.

It is now 8:00, and we are at least half an hour away from the spur trail to the Fort Ancient museum, the only shelter we anticipate along the trail ahead. We quicken our pace, find the spur trail to Fort Ancient, hike up the hill as sprinkles encourage us along, and make our way through the ancient earthworks. The length of the earthworks must be at least half a mile; it takes us about 15 minutes to walk it, and we take some time to stop for pictures.

The museum normally opens at 10 a.m., but a groundskeeper is using a weed-whacker outside, and while we are talking, his supervisor calls and agrees to allow us to enter at 9:15. By 9:45, the zero percent chance of rain has changed from sprinkles into a downpour. What a great place to wait out the storm!

We watch a DVD about Fort Ancient and study the displays. We are told to think of the area not as a fort but as a church that includes astronomical alignments, burial areas, and ceremonial spaces. The walls, originally constructed circa 100 BC with 84 openings or gateways, are currently 23 feet high and are estimated to have been 27 feet tall before centuries of erosion took a toll.

The Hopewell Indians cut trees and planted grain, and they brought in clay to line ponds to capture and hold rainwater on top of the hill. It is estimated that one million cubic yards of soil was moved. The ponds are also ringed by limestone, and there are roads or pathways of flat limestone leading out from some of the gates to waterways, perhaps for people arriving by the river. The north entrance has a 500-foot, limestone-paved "road" that passes between twin mounds. Archaeologists continue to learn more about the area as our technology for scanning underground features improves.

The zero-percent-chance storm event finally ends at 3:00 in the afternoon. We load up, say goodbye to the staff who have become good friends during our unexpected six-hour stay, and head down to the trail on the bike path.

The rain event has changed our plans. We had intended to enjoy a leisurely canoe float down the Little Miami River this afternoon. However, it's too late for that; so instead of camping at a canoe livery, we hike farther on to Waynesville.

Along the way, I make a call to Lori, in the next town up. Andy Niekamp, who thru-hiked the BT in 2011, is very active in the local hiking organization and "spilled the beans" about our hike. He told members to contact us if they thought they could help us out in any way. Lori sent us a note offering assistance.

Lori drives a few miles to pick us up at a trailhead along the bike trail, and we land in a lovely home and have a do-it-yourself salad with a delicious choice of fixings. Lori is a single mom, a recent "empty nester," and works in the computer world. She has begun making some life changes: purchasing this home in a new town and expanding her comfort zone to do things that she has not done. Accepting us into her home is one of those moves. We are happy for her choice, as we are able to have a warm shower, do our laundry, have a comfortable bed—and make a new friend.

While we are eating, a friend of Lori's stops over and joins us for a salad. The two friends make plans for tomorrow: bicycle to Yellow

Springs Street Festival, do one hour of kayaking, and complete the day with an evening bicycle ride. Quite a full and active schedule!

We have completed another section of the BT today—we left the Loveland Section and began the Caesar Creek Section.

Day 51: June 11, Saturday

Hiker midnight was ignored last night. We were up late, talking with Lori and finishing the day's journal. Bedtime was 10:15. So this morning, we struggle to rally ourselves at 6 a.m.

Lori offers to cook eggs for breakfast, but the cold cereal is fine, since we rarely have access to it while hiking. After last-minute photos and goodbyes, we walk out Lori's door onto the bikeway 50 feet away and head north.

The highs today will be in the 90s. Dew glistens on horsetail rushes and spider webs along the trail. I try to capture the images.

An hour and forty-five minutes later, we are crossing under the notorious U.S. 35. If you remember, a couple of weeks ago we were crossing underneath the same U.S. 35 through a concrete tunnel with a gazillion ticks on either side. Today is so much tamer—we travel on a paved bike path underneath the high, arching highway bridges.

In Xenia, around 9:15 a.m., we make a top at the restored railway station to use the restrooms and refill water bottles. In the downtown area, we veer off the trail at the courthouse and walk about three blocks to the post office, where we buy a small box to ship some things back home. Each of us contributes two and a half pounds of clothing, water purification equipment, and personal gear we are certain we no longer need. (We never used the water filtration system on our hike. Generous people have supplied water.) Beth's pack now weighs 16.5 pounds and mine weighs about 25 pounds with a couple of days of food.

SOUTHERN TERMINUS

Xenia Station

Heading north out of Xenia (population 25,879), we pass Shawnee Park, a lovely city park with a large, covered bandstand and a pond with a fountain. On this warm day, the park is already a busy place. We don't hike too far before we meet Lori and her friend, out for their morning bicycle ride. We have a short chat, again thank Lori for her hospitality, and part to pursue our own schedules for the day. At a gas station food mart, we purchase protein bars, crackers, cookies, V8 drinks, and a coffeecake—calories and liquid for another few miles.

I call Apple, and he tells us he is bicycling between Xenia and Yellow Springs. Eventually we find him waiting by the trail for us. We had considered asking him for a ride to a restaurant and motel this evening and a pickup tomorrow morning, but we now have a contact in Yellow Springs who offered us a campsite in their back yard (again, thanks to Andy Niekamp's announcement about our hike.) So we tell Apple we'll have to postpone his services until another time, but we make tentative plans to meet him in a few days, either on Tuesday or

Wednesday—whichever day has the highest forecast for rain. Then we three will tour the National Air Force museum in Dayton. We look forward to this—Apple has a lighthearted view of life and is a delight to be with.

Even though we're using our umbrellas, we feel the effects of the 90-plus-degree, energy-sapping, afternoon heat as we walk along the paved bikeway.

We are still a mile away from downtown Yellow Springs (population 3,513) when we encounter cars parked alongside the road and people walking to and from the street festival. The Yellow Springs Street Fair is held twice a year and draws well over 20,000 people. We find booths of every craft imaginable and begin walking down the rows, taking in the scene, but also looking for one booth in particular.

At the Yellow Springer T-shirt booth, we stop and meet Mark Heise, his wife, Robin, and their daughter, Morgan. Mark is our Yellow Springs contact we received from the local hiking club.

With Mark Heise at Yellow Springs Street Fair

SOUTHERN TERMINUS

We learn a little bit about the inkjet process Mark uses to create his beautiful T-shirts. He offers us cold, bottled water, which we gratefully down in quick order. An active member of the BTA, Mark will be coordinating next year's annual Buckeye TrailFest. (The 2017 TrailFest will be held in Yellow Springs.)

Hunger leads our conversation to restaurants, and Mark recommends the Current Cuisine. We take his recommendation and discover an excellent deli, where we nourish ourselves with a couple of different salads, including two pounds of fruit salad—perfect for this steamy, hot day. Dessert? Ice cream, of course. At a gasoline food mart, we purchase a pint and easily consume it.

Walking back from our meal, we chance upon a booth where a lady named Space is selling specialty soaps. Beth knows of these products; she first learned about them at a tea house/coffee shop in Athens, Ohio, when we were there to meet with Andrew Bashaw. Beth was impressed by the soap products and thinks they are among the best. She had never met Space, but they communicated via email, and so this chance meeting today is exciting.

Space and her husband were from Southern California and hitchhiked across the U.S. in their younger years. When she got to Athens, Ohio, she said, "I have found my home." They set up residence there and raised three children.

While we are talking with Space, Brent Anslinger stops by the booth. We know him from the Buckeye TrailFest two years ago. He and his wife, Amy, thru-hiked the BT in 2003, before the Wilderness Loop had been completed (2005). We exchange a few stories about the trail, but there is not enough time for many details. The Anslingers are younger than Beth and I and were able to hike 25 to 30 miles a day. They started their hike at the southern terminus in Cincinnati in September and completed the hike by mid-November. Ticks were not a problem for them, but they had to deal with colder weather.

The trail, of course, has changed over the last 13 years, but a thru-hike of this length, at any time, is a commendable accomplishment. The list of people who have thru-hiked the Buckeye Trail Big Loop is still fairly short:

2000 John Merrill – England (wrote a book: *A Walk in Ohio*)
2003 Brent & Amy Anslinger – Miamisburg, OH
2004 Peter & Joyce Cottrell – Whitefield, NH
2011 Andy Niekamp – Dayton, OH
2012 Denise "Ladybug" Hill – Cincinnati, OH
2013 Mary Warren and Lisa Strohm – Lancaster, OH

This year, 2016, may be a banner year; we have heard that a couple of other people may also thru-hike the trail this summer or fall.

Beth and I have completed our long distance hikes by simply moving forward, one step at time. For me, long-distance hiking is comparable to moving piles of dirt or to building a retaining wall. The seemingly insurmountable tasks are accomplished one shovelful, one stone, and one step at a time. The task may make the body weary and sore, but you will sleep well at night and bask in a glow when the time comes to sit back and enjoy the labor that has been completed.

When the street fair is over, Mark and Robin Heise quickly disassembled their T-shirt booth and pack it into their trailer and cars. Their home is only a mile up the road. Their dog is using the backyard, and the busy road runs in front of the house, so Mark suggests we find a comfortable corner inside for our mats. Thus we find ourselves indoors again, with a wonderful shower after a really hot, sweaty day.

Day 52: June 12, Sunday

We are up by 5 a.m., packed, and out the door at 5:25. In pre-dawn light, we walk back to the center of Yellow Springs. After the chaos of the festival yesterday, the town is very quiet.

We stop at a new motel in town to pick up information for the databook. As we leave Yellow Springs, darkness begins to lift and the eastern sky blazes with a spectacular combination of clouds and color. Streaks of sunlight cast long shadows over the gently rolling fields of corn and soybeans. The temperature is already at 73 degrees and is forecasted to rise into the 80s today—better than the low-90s of yesterday, but still hot.

Early Morning Road Walk

Passing by a small farm wood lot, we hear a low growl that can only come from a large animal. I have no idea what that large animal may be, but its growl is definitely more fearsome than our "bobcat" sounds. Is it a bear? Some other creature? I've never heard anything like it, but the sound is what I would expect from a large cat—such as a cougar—but that would be very unusual. I do know there have been sightings of Bigfoot in Ohio. I am going with that one.

The walk from Yellow Springs to Fairborn/Dayton is a road walk and will take us out of the Caesar Creek Section and into the Troy Section of the BT. There are few trees along the way to provide shade, and we can feel the increasing power of the rising sun, making an early start almost a necessity. In Fairborn, we pause at a gas station food mart to make use of the restrooms, fill our water bottles, and buy V8 drink and trail mix.

Joining a bikeway, we soon encounter a major engineering feat—one of five specially built dams on the Miami River. Instead of constructing permanent impoundments to control flooding, the Miami Conservancy District (MCD) chose to build dams that allow the river to flow freely through an opening at the bottom. During a flood event, the excess water piles up behind the narrow constriction of the dam and floods land that has been purposefully set aside for such events. The construction allows only a specified amount of water to be discharged through the bottom opening; and as the water recedes, the river returns to its normal flow pattern.

In a few miles, we pass the entrance to Wright State University, and about three miles farther, we pass the entrance to the National Museum of the U.S. Air Force. Our current plan is to return with Apple to the museum on Wednesday.

Next to the trail is a Comfort Suites hotel, and inside we find root beer and snacks and an air-conditioned lobby to cool our overheated bodies. The outside temperature is 85 degrees in the shade, with a "feel" temperature of 90 degrees. The lobby host is friendly and takes an interest in our hike. We have a pleasant conversation with him. It's tempting to linger in the cool air, but we need to go seven more miles.

Soon after we leave the Comfort Suites, we follow the blue blazes off the bike path and onto a footpath along the Mad River. The water is moving along nicely and invites us in for a canoe ride or perhaps a splash in a refreshing pool. However, we must decline the invitation and press on another mile.

We go through a park and cross a lagoon, following the bicycle trail. In another mile, a sign warns us, TRAIL CLOSED.

Stopping a bicyclist, I ask if we can proceed on the trail. He tells us the construction is for a new road bridge across the Mad River, which we have been following, and assures us it is possible to walk across the site and continue on the trail. He also tells us to "watch for the large fountains that shoot up on the hour." The fountains are an attraction in Deeds Point MetroPark, located at the confluence of the Great Miami and Mad Rivers near downtown Dayton.

SOUTHERN TERMINUS

We note that it is nearly 3 p.m. and thank him for the information. Soon, on the horizon, we can see large jets of water shooting into the air, even though Deeds Point is still two miles away.

We have no trouble crossing the construction zone; it is Sunday, and no work is in progress. When we arrive at Deeds Point, we have about 20 minutes before the fountain operates again.

We walk around the park, take our pictures with statues of Orville and Wilbur Wright, and read a couple of plaques about the grass airfields that used to exist in the area for early flight tests. The Wright brothers began flying at Huffman Prairie in 1904. However, after 105 flights, they had logged a total of less than 50 minutes in the air. The next year also began poorly, with erratic flights and crash landings. After Orville survived a frightening crash in July, the brothers made changes. They incorporated all they had learned into a new plane and in late August unveiled the Wright Flyer III. With the new plane, they were able to consistently fly multiple circles over the prairie.

With Orville & Wilbur Wright

At the junction of the Great Miami and Mad Rivers, five structures are located on the riverbanks and a center structure is situated in the water. When the fountain begins to operate, giant jets of water, perhaps 6 to 8 inches in diameter, shoot out 400 feet from the five structures on land, and the center structure in the river shoots a large column of water 200 feet into the air with a ring of smaller jets of water. Mist fills the air and the grand sight lasts about 10 minutes.

Fountain at Deeds Point, Dayton

Later, I consult the Internet and learn that the fountain system is equipped with directional wind sensors. If the wind is blowing in a direction and at a velocity that could interfere with area traffic or other activities, individual jets of the fountain will not operate. Also, during the cold months when freezing water could create hazardous conditions on nearby roads and recreation trails, the fountain is turned off. The fountain was installed in 2001 when the park opened. The five streams of water symbolize the five regional rivers and the giant center spray honors the region's abundance of water. We are told that at night the fountain spires are bathed in lights that create almost every color imaginable.

The bike path and the BT leave Deeds Point and eventually go through the lovely Island MetroPark. On this hot, beautiful Sunday afternoon, it is very popular.

We cross a footbridge over the Great Miami River and within a couple of miles divert up a street to the Hotel Dayton on Wagner Ford Road, less than two miles away. Along the way, two young adults give us a sob story about needing a dollar for bus fare. I give it to them, but know they will be spending it on alcohol. Sure enough, within a few blocks we look back, and they are coming out of a store and carrying a brown paper bag.

At the motel, we check in, take showers, and order Domino's Pizza, whose number is listed on the hotel room key. The service is quick; within 30 minutes we have more pizza than we can eat. We save some for tomorrow.

Our hike today was 25.8 miles, and we found that going through Dayton on the bicycle path is quite pleasant, since the blue blazes lead through numerous parks.

Chapter 8

MIAMI & ERIE CANAL NORTHBOUND

Day 53: June 13, Monday

One of the advantages of a big city is the availability of taxi service, and after last night's experience with the panhandlers, we make arrangements for a morning cab ride back to the hike-bike path.

Today will be a shorter hike, which allows time to enjoy a 6:30 breakfast at the motel. Then it's a short cab ride to the trail.

The hike-bike path passes a golf course where the grass wears a heavy, silvery dew and long tree shadows stretch across the morning landscape. The scene touches a primordial part of me—it looks and feels like sunrise on the open savannas of Africa.

In a wooded section, the trail does not go in a straight line; rather, it gently curves around tall trees and green and lush undergrowth, as though wandering through a garden setting. Vibrant floral colors are the only missing element.

The path crosses a bridge over the Great Miami River, and we now enjoy a walk along its banks. We spot geese and mallards, watch the riffles over shallow, gravel areas, and hear the river inviting us to splash around or float a canoe on its waters.

A momentous event: At 8:35 a.m., we cross under I-70, heading north! We are now on the north side of I-70 once again. The last time we were north of this interstate highway was 38 days ago (on May 6).

After passing under U.S. 40, we find a historic marker that tells the story of the highway called "The National Road":

Authorized by Congress in 1806, the National Road was the nation's first federally funded interstate highway. National leaders desired an all-weather road across the Allegheny Mountains in order to develop closer political and economic ties between the east and west. Considered to be a significant engineering feat, the Road opened Ohio and much of the old Northwest Territory to settlement, provided access for Ohio goods to reach eastern markets, and enabled Ohio citizens to play important roles in the affairs of the new nation. The National Road was renowned for the number of quality inns and taverns during the heyday of the stagecoach. The Road declined after 1850 as railroads became the preferred method of travel. The automobile, however, brought new life to the Road. Reborn as U.S. 40, it became a busy 24-hour-a-day artery, with truck stops, motor courts, and diners until superseded by the interstate highways in the 1960s.

✧ ✧

By noon, we are in Tipp City (population 9,809), a town that grew up along the Miami and Erie Canal. It is located at Lock 15, which is now dry, although the stonework is still in place.

A decaying canal boat rests close to Lock 15, and an old flour mill has been turned into a community building. A historic plaque reads:

> This section of the Miami and Erie Canal, constructed from 1833-1837, was vital to this region's commerce and development. It allowed for farmers and businesses to get their goods to larger markets at a lower cost and faster speed than by hauling overland. Passengers could also travel across the area by canal boat. John Clark saw the location of Lock 15, situated

in Monroe Township at the junction of the Milton-Carlisle Pike (Main Street), as an opportunity and in 1840, platted the new town of Tippecanoe City (now Tipp City). Many types of commerce and trade grew up around the canal including boarding houses, saloons, a tannery, and a mill. Some of the original buildings still stand, such as a mill to the west of Lock 15, John Clark's home at the southeast corner of Main and First streets, and the hotel at the northeast corner of Main and Second streets.

Lock 15 – Tipp City

Travel on the Miami and Erie Canal was limited to four miles per hour for boats pulled by mules in order to prevent boat wash from eroding the clay banks of the canals. A system of locks allowed a canal boat to be raised or lowered, depending on the direction the boat was traveling. Constructed of limestone blocks, Lock 15 is typical of most Miami and Erie Canal locks. Large wooden gates were located on each end of the lock. A boat would enter the lock and the gate behind it would close, while the opposite gate would open, allowing the water level to be raised or lowered before the boat could proceed to its next stop. The advent of the railroad was the beginning of the end for the canal system. Due to extensive damage, most of the Miami and Erie Canal was abandoned following the Great Flood of 1913.

We turn into the historic portion of Tipp City, where Beth needs to find a restroom and goes into a real estate office. The people are polite and friendly, and one gentleman, Jim, offers us a ride to our motel about one and a half miles away near Interstate 75. In the blink of an eye, it seems, we are in our room and ready for a shower. Jim is now among our growing list of trail angels.

I notify Andy Niekamp and Mike Fanelli of our arrival and arrange to meet them for dinner at 4 p.m. Across the street, I buy a couple of items at the gas station food mart and then, back in our room, write journal notes until our friends arrive.

Andy and Mike are both BTA members and involved with hiking, trail maintenance, and promoting the trail. We first came to know Andy at the 2014 Buckeye TrailFest when we attended his presentation on his 2011 BT thru-hike. Mike is involved with Boy Scouts and has also made presentations at each Buckeye TrailFest.

We have a leisurely dinner with Andy and Mike at Frisch's Big Boy near our hotel. We have much to talk about regarding our mutual experiences on the trail, the condition of the trail, people we have met along the hike, and Andy's efforts to provide us with contacts in this area from the meet-up group he created about seven years ago. The group has grown to nearly 3,000 members, thanks in part to the power of social media. We could converse all night, but Mike has a meeting to attend, and we have an early departure tomorrow.

Once again, conversation and sharing experiences with other hikers has been very refreshing.

Day 54: June 14, Tuesday

This morning, the La Quinta motel accommodates us by putting out breakfast food at 5:30 a.m., half an hour earlier than their normal start time. We take advantage of their generosity until the "World's Best Trail Angel" shows up at 6 a.m.

Apple shuttles us back to the trail at Lock 15 and bids farewell as we head north. His plan for the day is to drive to the Arrowston Bed and Breakfast in Piqua with Beth's backpack and some of our equipment, giving us another welcome slackpack day. I keep my backpack, with just the minimal food, water, rain jackets, and umbrellas for our 18.2-mile hike. After making our delivery to the B&B, Apple will then bicycle south on the bike path, so we will meet him again somewhere on the trail today.

The morning sunrise paints the sky a lovely turquoise in a beautiful pattern of multi-layered clouds. An attractive hike-bike path generally follows the old Miami and Erie Canal. We cross lovely bridges over rivers and pass Lock 14 and two aqueducts, structures built to carry the canal across side streams entering the Great Miami River. At the second aqueduct, the water in the stream is so clear that we can see the foundation timbers used to control the erosive power of the stream and protect the aqueduct's stone walls. The engineering design that went into the canal is quite a marvel for the 1830s.

Bridge on Bike Trail

A rabbit darts across the bike path, and then in a few steps we see that it has joined its friend in a grassy area to enjoy a morning meal.

On our approach to the small city of Troy (population 25,445), the skyline is dominated by the county courthouse, its high dome looking like a miniature U.S. Capitol building.

This is where we also cross paths with Apple, on his way down from Piqua, and we stop to chat a bit. He is going to bike farther south before turning around. Even so, he does overtake us again as we are approaching some ball fields north of Troy. We exchange small talk and make plans for meeting in the city of Piqua.

We cross the Great Miami River at Troy and a couple more times on our way to Piqua. The hike-bike bridges over the Great Miami River have been beautifully constructed.

Around noon, clouds begin to fill the sky and provide shade from the noonday heat.

A plaque entitled "The Atomic City" tells an interesting story about Piqua:

> In the 1960s, the city of Piqua was known worldwide as the "Atomic City." Piqua was the site chosen in 1957 by the Atomic Energy Commission to build the world's first nuclear reactor to produce electricity for a city. Harnessing atomic energy became a reality, first, in war, only 12 years earlier. By the mid-1950s, a nuclear reactor was providing power for a submarine, the U.S.S. Nautilus. A giant aircraft carrier, the U.S.S. Enterprise was under construction and was expected to launch around 1960. It, too, was to be powered by nuclear energy. At the same time that our military was exploring nuclear energy as a way to power warships, our government was looking for ways to put the power of the atom to use to light America's cities.

Construction on Piqua's reactor began with the 1959 groundbreaking. The average person in Piqua, and in America, knew little about atomic energy at that time. The most-known fact was the destruction of Hiroshima and Nagasaki in August of 1945. Meetings were held to alleviate fears, but some still had concerns. There are reports of people being concerned that nuclear particles might travel down the electric wires into homes, contaminating citizens. These fears were, of course, without merit.

The project, funded by the federal government, was completed at a cost of $7.7 million dollars. By November 1962, Piqua was truly, "The Atomic City," as the reactor came online and began producing electricity. It was estimated that the energy produced by 260 pounds of enriched uranium would equal that produced by 160 million pounds of coal.

The city received 20 percent of its electric power from the reactor until it was closed down in December 1967. The "experiment" had proven a success.

The paved hike-bike route through Piqua is along a route that had been an old railway, situated on an elevated mound of dirt that has since been removed to street level; hence, there are no buildings of historical value near the trail, and our trip through Piqua (population 20,699) is rather uneventful. We exit the town at the northwest end and arrive at our destination, the Arrowston Inn Bed & Breakfast, operated by Norman and Georgia Armstrong.

It is 1 p.m., and I text Apple. He responds that he will be here in 10 minutes.

Lunch is the first order of business. We ask for a restaurant recommendation, and the Armstrongs suggest Beppo Uno Pizzeria.

Apple arrives, cheerful as ever, drives us into Piqua, and joins us for our late lunch. While we are inside enjoying the good food, heavy clouds swiftly move in and rain pours down for 45 minutes.

The Arrowston Inn must be one of the grandest homes now used for a bed and breakfast. After we take a shower, our hosts guide us around the "museum-quality" home. The original home was built in 1887 by William K. Boal, who owned the Favorite Stove and Range manufacturing company (we had seen a plaque along the trail that told us a little bit about the company). The house is a three-story home and more to the Georgian style. It is listed in the U.S. National Register of Historic Places.

Norman Armstrong is a retired doctor and acquired the home in 1990. Until they began renovations, the Armstrongs were unaware that under the carpet in the foyer was a floor made of inlaid, 12-inch squares of black and white Italian marble. They also found that other rooms had beautiful inlaid hardwood floors. After the renovation, the Armstrongs had pictures taken of the individual rooms and sent the photos to a furniture manufacturer, requesting that appropriate furniture be constructed for each room. Next, an interior designer suggested artwork for each room. Without a doubt, the house is a beautiful home.

We sit in the library and talk, mainly about breeding and raising race horses—Norman's passion during 1987-88. We also learn more about the inn's history. The Fruit of the Loom Company was established in Piqua, and Johnny Wiessmuller, Olympic swimmer and "Tarzan" actor, was a model for Fruit of the Loom products and stayed at this private home during his visits to Piqua, swimming laps every morning in the outdoor, full-size swimming pool. In the 1950s, other famous guests included Bing Crosby, Frank Sinatra, Bob Hope, and Doc Severinsen.

Sadly, Norman's health is not the best, and he prefers living in Florida. The house is being sold, and this is the last week that it will be operated as a bed and breakfast. We feel fortunate to have the opportunity to stay in this home.

In our room hangs a picture of two glass swans, head-to-head, their outlines forming a heart. The quote above it reads, *Each of us is half ... incomplete; together we are as one heart.*

A long journey such as this hike has its adversities and long stretches of isolation, but also moments of stunning beauty and exciting events. These Beth and I have shared, and they bring the quote to life.

On this hike and ever since we met, Beth makes it easy to be the love of my life. She laughs at my goofy comments and expresses her appreciation for everything I do for her (and even just for being here). I believe she has said thanks for every meal we have had together and every day we have been together. While I will try to express my appreciation, it seems to flow more easily from her. I also see this appreciation expressed whenever we meet people along the way and someone does the smallest kindness for us, even when that kindness is just part of their job.

Our lives intertwined when we were both able to be retired, and we've been able to be together nearly every moment since we met.

Day 55: June 15, Wednesday
Georgia serves breakfast at 8 a.m., and our hosts entertain us with stories of doctoring, the house, and Piqua.

Today is a zero day, though we will be doing some walking because Apple is taking us to the National Air Force Museum. He really enjoys the museum and will be our personal guide. The drive to the museum takes nearly an hour, which impresses on us how far we have hiked since passing the museum three days ago.

We are all anticipating a tour of the new presidential wing, opened just a few days ago, and we head there first. Air Force One planes are on display—from the very first airplane used by Truman up to Nixon's jet. Beth and I play "First Couple" on the steps of an Air Force One plane, waving to our loyal followers below (I think Apple is the only one), and Beth emails the photo to family members.

Air Force One

The section also houses many types of research and development (R&D) planes, old rockets, and a full-size shuttle trainer.

We bypass parts of the museum housing the information on WWI and WWII.

My personal interest is in early flight development. We start with a guided, 45-minute tour at 1:30. There is so much to absorb that we stay an additional hour to watch an eight-minute video and read the display information. The section includes reproductions of the Wright flyer, the Curtis plane, and other planes developed within 10 to 20 years of the Wright brothers' first flight.

The Wright brothers became interested in flying in 1895. After reading most of the literature on flight available at the time, they hit upon the idea of warping the wings for lateral control. A 5-foot span biplane kite was built in 1899 to test the idea. Building on their experience with the kite, they constructed a 17-foot glider in the fall of 1900; and in 1901, a 22-foot glider. Those tests were at Kill Devil Hills in North Carolina. The wings did not provide the lift promised in existing data tables, so they built a wind tunnel to create better data tables for airfoil lift and drag—a milestone that led to their success in building a true flying machine.

Patent lawsuits and other business matters prevented the Wright brothers from developing the plane beyond the Model C. In addition, the U.S. government was a little slow in picking up the importance of aviation, and Europe quickly took the lead in aeronautical developments for a few years. Such matters took their toll on Wilbur's health, and in 1912, he died after contracting typhoid fever. Eating bad seafood on a business trip to Boston may also have played a role in his death. Orville died in 1948 at the age of 76. He had seen America go from the horse and buggy to the supersonic age.

We finish our museum tour at 3:45 and head back to Piqua. Dinner is at Mulligan's Pub, where Beth and I both have salads and Apple has chicken nuggets and fries.

Once again, while we are in a restaurant, a storm cell dumps a torrential amount of rain. In a brief interlude, we dash out to the car and arrive back at the Arrowston Inn before another storm cell descends upon us. We are fortunate and grateful to be inside.

Day 56: June 16, Thursday

Today also starts a little later. Breakfast is at 8:30, with delicious quiche, fresh fruit, and apple cobbler.

We are going to visit the Johnston Farm & Indian Agency, and we take advantage of the "Apple transportation service" to the historic farm. Our friend joins us for a tour.

John Johnston was born on March 25, 1775, in Ireland. He came to America at age 11 and by age 16 had a business, selling and transporting supplies to forts on the American frontier. He liked the upper Piqua area near the Great Miami River and purchased land there in 1804. This would become his "gentleman's farm" and his family's home. He was also operating a trading post in Fort Wayne, Indiana, and served as an Indian agent for the U.S. government, earning the trust of the tribes he served. He was one of the first commissioners who were responsible for choosing the route of the Miami and Erie

Canal, which, unsurprisingly enough, goes through his farm. The Johnstons had 15 children, 14 of whom lived into adulthood. John Johnston died in February of 1861, one month before the Civil War broke out.

The farm presents scenes of farming, canal transportation, and Native American history. The farmhouse, completed in 1815, is a three-story, brick Federal. It served as both a home and an Indian agency. The bricks were made in kilns on the property. A two-story springhouse (with the original spring still running through it) was not only the source of water and the method of cooling and storing food, but it also had space for textile production, the making of lye soap and candles, and a loft where hired hands slept. Johnston cultivated an extensive apple orchard, and hard and soft cider was made in the cider house, a building that no longer exists but has been recreated.

A two-mile section of the canal has been restored, and a canal boat operates for a fee. The boat is a 70-foot replica of the canal boats used for transportation of passengers and cargo in the nineteenth century. With a team of mules plodding along the towpath and a costumed narrator accompanying us, we enjoy a leisurely trip from days of old. The boat glides quietly along the waterway as the scenery slips past.

Chuck with Trail Angel "Apple"

Back on the trail, we bid goodbye to Apple. He has given so much of his time, not only in helping us along our way but also in assisting many other hikers on several trails over the past 15 years. This is the most time that we have spent with him, and he is now not only our trail angel but also our good friend. He has a great sense of humor, likes to laugh, and seems to enjoy life. We had 48 hours with him, and it is hard to say goodbye; but we have 13 miles to hike to a shelter. We truly look forward to meeting up with him again.

We get underway by 2 p.m.

The trail, now a dirt footpath, takes us past Lock 8, which we had seen from the canal boat. In a couple of miles we pass Lock 7, turn off the towpath and onto a road, and hike to the town of Lockington (population 140). This is at the highest elevation of the canal, and at one time, a "staircase" of six locks located here moved boats up or down 67 feet over a distance of just 2,800 feet.

Lockington Locks

A little past Lockington, we climb to the top of the earthen portion of a Miami Conservancy District flood control dam and then pick up the towpath for another two miles. The towpath trail so far has been nicely mowed and maintained, although there are poison ivy patches that cannot be avoided.

Back on a road for six miles, we pass a plaque about the first brick house built in Shelby County, by John Wilson in 1816. We can see the house, about 800 feet in the distance. The two-story home, with the original log cabin still adjacent, was in serious disrepair until the entire farm was purchased in 2006 by an individual who restored the home and brought its history alive. Once a center of commerce for the surrounding area and an important stop on the Underground Railroad, it is now on the National Register of Historic Places.

A couple of miles later, we cross the General Harmar Military Trail of 1790.

Native American tribes traveled through the region on the rivers and by following the trails initially cut by animals moving to salt licks and river crossings. Of the 31 documented Indian trails in Ohio, two cross Shelby County. One, known as the "Miami Trail," was used by General Harmar and his troops in 1790, when he marched against a tribal confederation led by Miami Chief Michikinikwa (known as Little Turtle). Harmar was defeated and eventually returned to Philadelphia and retired from the military in 1792.

It is quite windy today. Perhaps it is because we have arrived in the flatland of northwest Ohio, and as the saying goes, "the only thing between you and Canada is a fence—and it is blown down." The sky is overcast, and we do not require much water for our hike.

We pass a field of amber, waving grain, which creates a brilliant contrast to the surrounding green woods and hay fields. Finally, we turn onto the towpath for our last 1.2 miles, arriving at a shelter at 6:45 in the evening. A small metal plate in the shelter reads as follows:

> Parker A. Cole
> Troop 95, Sidney, Ohio
> Eagle Scout project
> September 2009

Each shelter along our hike has presented us with an upgrade in accommodations, and this, our third shelter, was built by a Scout and is quite nice. However, I think it is too tall and the opening to the wind and rain too large.

Not much to do but the usual—journal and get to sleep by 8:45.

Boy Scout Shelter

Day 57: June 17, Friday

When a couple hikes together as we are doing, it's important for each to care for the comfort and safety of the other. Our days always begin with a morning kiss and end with a goodnight kiss, reassuring each other that all is well. Despite days that might be stressful and difficult, we know that each will look out for the other, no matter what situation we face.

One of the joys in being with Beth is her genuine appreciation for everything that is done for her. Whether it is a motel, dinner, or something as simple as an ice cream cone or a can of pop, she will nearly always say thank you with a kiss.

As a matter of routine, Beth likes for me to lift the pack onto her back. I load up my pack, and she checks the straps on the front of my pack that have a habit of working themselves loose. A quick look around our campsite ensures we are leaving nothing behind. Once on the trail, Beth prefers that I take the lead. A dubious honor, since I have to break all the cobwebs!

We are on the trail at 6:25 a.m.

Even though the towpath is mowed and branches are periodically clipped back, poison ivy and nettles are persistently prevalent, so long pants are recommended.

Towpath

We have a cloudless morning, and a light breeze keeps us pleasantly cool.

The dirt towpath trail is supposed to cross State Route 66 and continue north, but a major footbridge has collapsed and the trail is closed. The detour takes us up State Route 66 for a ways before turning onto another road to pick up the towpath.

When I pause to make notes for the databook, Beth does not always wait; rather, she just marches ahead and I then have to jog a little to reach her again. At other times, she turns and waits for me to catch up. We do not like to be out of each other's sight—at least, not very long. This is not only for the sake of safety; it's also nice to know that someone is within earshot when a comment must be made or a view needs to be shared. This is, perhaps, is one of the best joys of having a partner on a hike—your experiences are shared and become a part of your life together.

Upon arriving in Fort Loramie (population 1,497) around 10:30 a.m., we take a break in the park gazebo. The downtown is quite small but very neat, and most of the buildings appear to be well maintained.

While I write notes, Beth heads across the street to a hardware store, hoping to replace a pair of reading glasses that slipped out of her pack somewhere. She finds no glasses, but does see items that could be part of a resupply—nuts, trail mix, and the like. The store also has Grandma's Poison Ivy Soap, made in Tulsa, Oklahoma. The sales clerk sells a bar to Beth, claiming that rubbing it on skin before going into the woods prevents contracting poison ivy, washing with it removes poison ivy oils already on one's skin, and making a lather of it and leaving it to dry on a poison ivy rash will speed up healing.

We walk over to the Dairy King for an early lunch of fish sandwiches, fries, drinks, and a soft pretzel to go. I enjoy a strawberry custard ice cream cone. I don't think I've ever heard of strawberry custard ice cream before. They also have a pop machine that dispenses 12-ounce cans for 50 cents!

By noon, we are walking into the Fort Loramie State Park campground. It is Father's Day weekend, and the campground is completely booked, although some walk-in sites are available. We had only 11 miles to hike today, so we have a leisurely afternoon to shower, do laundry, and relax in the heat of the day. Our campsite is next to a small arm of the lake.

While people continuously flow in, some have already set up and are cooking meals over open fires. Fortunately, we are upwind of any campfire smoke. Unfortunately, most campers are not interested in hiker midnight (8 p.m.), so it will be noisy for a couple of hours and the best we can do is lie down and rest.

Fort Loramie State Park Campground

Day 58: June 18, Saturday

We are up at 5:45 a.m. and on the trail by 6:15. The trail starts off, heading north to a feeder canal that runs west from Loramie Lake to the Miami and Erie Canal.

Built in sections, the Miami and Erie Canal was finally completed from the Ohio River to Lake Erie in 1845. It was 248.8 miles long and rose 512 feet from the Ohio River to the Loramie Summit (a 23-mile flat stretch) before descending 395 feet to Lake Erie. The canal had 103 locks, 19 aqueducts, 3 reservoirs, and 3 guard locks. The waterway was 28 feet wide at the bottom and 40 feet wide at the top, with a water depth of 4 feet. Alongside the canal, the towpath was 10 feet wide. In 1851, at the peak of operation, about 400 boats were using this method of transportation.

This portion of the Buckeye Trail is wooded for about one mile. Once it reaches the main canal, we walk through grass and then along a cornfield for another mile. The morning sky is clear, but the sun has not had time to dry the dew from the grass and our pant legs are soon soaked. However, the two-mile road walk into Minster (population 2,800) is sufficient to dry our clothes.

Beyond Minster, we hike for three miles on a hike-bike path surfaced with crushed limestone. The old canal is to our right and has not been dewatered; the stagnant water is covered with green duckweed, fallen logs lie in the water, and noisy bullfrogs croak on the canal's banks.

For one mile leading into the town of New Bremen (population 2,983), a Boy Scout has placed five plaques along the canal with short historical facts about the Miami and Erie.

New Bremen takes its name from the town of the same name in Germany. In the 1830s, ships sailed between Bremen, Germany, and the United States. German immigrants could disembark in Baltimore, Maryland, travel through the mountains of Pennsylvania on the National Road (now known as U.S. Route 40) to Wheeling, West Virginia, and then continue by boat on the Ohio River to Cincinnati, Ohio. In Cincinnati, a group of Germans formed "The City of Bremen Society" on July 23, 1832. A charter was drawn up among the 33 members, authorizing the purchase of land for a Protestant town. Two hired scouts explored parts of western Ohio and eastern Indiana for suitable land before making the purchase of 80 acres at the site of what would become New Bremen. The plot of "Bremen" was officially recorded on June 11, 1833, and the name was changed to "New Bremen" in 1835, when it was determined that another town in Ohio was already named Bremen.

The canal quickly became the focal point of commerce for the growing town. The town is at Lock 1 North, which is the northern end of the 23-mile Loramie Summit plateau. Lock 1 was originally built of wood, due to the cost and difficulty of obtaining stone, but it was rebuilt in 1910 using concrete.

The town looks spotless, and buildings have been beautifully restored. A bicycle museum is west of the trail, and the New Bremen Coffee Café is about one block farther west. We arrive at the café at 9 a.m.; they have the perfect breakfast—spinach quiche with a muffin and small bowl of cut fruit. In this hot weather, we have enjoyed every opportunity where fruit of different varieties is available.

Bicycle Museum

For over an hour, we tour the Bicycle Museum of America, the largest collection of bicycles in the world. Previously located at the Navy Pier in Chicago, the collection was purchased by Jim Dicke of Crown Equipment Corporation, an international manufacturer of electric lift trucks, and brought to his hometown of New Bremen. The museum houses bicycles from the nineteenth century, balloon-tire classics, banana-seat high-rise handlebar bikes, and many more.

Before leaving New Bremen, we stop in a local pharmacy and this time Beth successfully replaces her lost reading glasses.

On the north end of town, we pass a city swimming pool and the Kuenning-Dicke Natural Area, which appears to be an old field that is intentionally left to transform through natural succession into a wooded area. Within that area, near the trail, is a new sleeping shelter that looks very nice.

Soon the paved path ends, and we are on a grass path once again. We must remain vigilant; poison ivy grows along the path here, too.

Towpath and Stone Milepost

A few original stone mileposts, marking the distance from Cincinnati, still exist along the canal. We pass mileposts 124, 125, 126, 127, and 128.

We also pass signs identifying sites where locks at one time existed. Most of those were wooden locks. Lock 8 is an exception. It is a beautiful stone structure, almost perfectly preserved, although it has been dewatered.

Lock 8 of Miami & Erie Canal

As we continue north, the canal remains on our right and fields of corn, soybeans, and hay are on our left. In one field, a farmer is running a machine to turn the hay so that it will dry uniformly.

Near the city of St. Marys (population 8,280), we pass over a feeder canal that carried water from Grand Lake St. Marys to the Miami and Erie. The lake was originally built as a reservoir to hold water used to maintain the water level in the canal. Walking into town at 3:20 p.m., we pass through Memorial Park, which has a replica of the *Belle of St. Marys,* a canal boat dry-docked on concrete supports within the old canal bed. A statue of a mule with a rope leading to the boat is also part of the display.

The park is memorable for us—at this point, we have crossed the 1,000-mile mark in our hike!

Our motel, America's Best Value Inn, is located 0.9 mile west of the trail, and we arrive there 20 minutes later. The motel receptionist is extremely friendly, and she is willing to help us out in any way possible. She lists the restaurants within a couple of blocks and informs us that the motel has their own lounge for drinks and pizza. When we notice that breakfast is not open until 6 a.m., she generously offers to let us take cold breakfast food up to our room for tomorrow morning. The motel gets high marks from us!

The pool looks very inviting on this stifling-hot day; but, as usual, I have notes to write in the journal and databook, and the temptation of a cool swim must be bypassed. A quick shower in the motel room will have to do.

It is too hot to walk to a restaurant, so we opt for root beer and pizza at the motel lounge. The food is really quite good.

I make a quick trip next door to the gas station food mart and buy a couple of snack items. We start each day with no more than one and a half days' worth of food because we are now finding several places to resupply at our stops along the way. However, carrying some food ensures that we can keep moving during the day, if necessary.

Day 59: June 19, Sunday

Mother Nature celebrates Father's Day with a special sunrise that brushes the eastern sky with a deep magenta. At 5:45 a.m., we leave the motel, walk back to the Buckeye Trail, and are again back on the canal towpath. Along the canal, we scare up ducks and watch as a carp churns the water violently upon our passing. We may have disturbed a muskrat or two, but we do not catch a glimpse of them.

About a mile up the towpath, we pass through a hiker tunnel that goes underneath U.S. 33. At the other end of the tunnel, the crushed limestone towpath gives way to a dirt and grass path. Fortunately, the path appears to have been mowed within the last couple of weeks, and we find it easy to walk.

At 8:20 a.m., we cross a bridge known as "Bloody Bridge." A plaque erected by the Auglaize County Historical Society in 1976 tells the story of two young men who competed for one girl by the name of Minnie. When Minnie chose one of them, the other took revenge in the fall of 1954. Carrying an ax, he met the couple on the bridge one night and killed the other man with one swing that severed his head. Minnie fell from the bridge and also died. The revenge-seeker disappeared; but a skeleton was found years later in a well, giving rise to much local speculation as to whether this was a suicide or justice.

Yesterday the temperature started in the 60s and climbed to 87. Today it started at 65 and reaches 90. Tomorrow's forecast is for even hotter temperatures. By 9 a.m., the sun has burned off the clouds and begins to burn down on us. Beth has already raised her "sunbrella," and within half an hour, I do the same.

At 10:30, we enter 20-acre Deep Cut Historical Park. This part of the canal construction required that a cut be made 6,660 feet long and up to 52 feet deep. The cut is through sand and gravel, so there is no dramatic rock cliff to let you know there is anything special about this section of the canal. The laborers who dug it were paid $0.30 per day with a jigger of whiskey to ward off disease, primarily malaria.

By 11:15, we have hiked the 14.5 miles to the small town of Spencerville (population 2,210). We arrive in town sooner than expected. Our destination was to be a shelter 4.5 miles from Spencerville, but now we look at Delphos as a possible destination. The town is 9.5 miles away—and it has a hotel! The promise of a shower and air conditioning is motivation enough to hike 24 miles on a steamy, hot day.

In Spencerville, a Subway restaurant associated with a Shell gas station is a temporary respite from the heat. We settle in, have a salad, and then make reservations at the only motel in Delphos (a Microtel).

Our Spencerville stop lasts 70 minutes, and then we are back on the trail, continuing on a flat, grassy path along the canal.

At 1:30 p.m., I see the temperature underneath the umbrella is 90 degrees. I hold the thermometer out in the sun—and it reads 106 degrees. Sixteen degrees is a significant difference in keeping the body temperature lower and not requiring us to drink so much water. We really love our umbrellas.

Towpath with Canal Lock Sign

We make reasonably good time to Delphos (population 7,044). In Delphos, we hitch a ride for the 1.3 miles off the trail to the motel. Our ride is with two young Mexicans who do not speak much English, and Beth happily converses in Spanish, making our request known. Once we are settled into the motel, we shower, find a restaurant that delivers, and place an order for fish nuggets, fries, and applesauce.

It is a late day for me; I complete journal and databook notes, make plans for tomorrow night, and reserve a hotel in Defiance for the following night.

Day 60: June 20, Monday

Oh, horrors! After a late night working, I do not wake up until 5:40 a.m. We hurriedly pack and go down to the motel's continental breakfast. We wanted to be out early this morning to beat the heat—the day is already starting off at 75 degrees.

We finally head out the door at 6:30—a time at which we should have had at least two to three miles already completed. We feel the warmth and humidity immediately.

Except for three or four miles, the walk today will be on roads. The highways now run straight and flat, and we can see a long way down the road. It is also very windy, and using the umbrellas is a challenge. I manage to find a way to use mine, but Beth, for the most part, walks without hers. The wind at least makes us "feel" cooler.

The corn here is about three feet tall, taller than we have seen previously. The farmers in this area may have been able to work their fields early and catch a couple of beneficial rains.

In the early morning, we hike through Fort Jennings (population 470). The town received its start and name from Colonel William Jennings, who, in September 1812, with his regiment of Kentucky Riflemen, was ordered by General W. H. Harrison to cut a road from Fort Barbee at St. Marys to a point midway to Defiance. The fort that Colonel Jennings established here was completed in October 1812, and the town of Fort Jennings was founded in 1847.

The next town is Ottoville (population 975), which has a beautiful red brick church with double spires that are visible from miles away. We stop briefly at a gas station food mart and purchase V8 juice, Sprite, protein bars, crackers, a donut, and ice cream.

By 10:25 a.m., we are on our way, and soon Beth spots a raccoon scurrying across the road. We have seen red-tailed hawks, blue herons, and a muskrat along the canal trail and sighted deer almost daily.

After about eight miles of road walk, we turn onto a three-mile stretch of towpath. Fortunately, someone has kept the path mowed; otherwise, it would obviously become quickly overgrown with grass, shrubs and lots of poison ivy.

Along the way, we encounter our first ripe black raspberries. We pick a half dozen but do not linger in the heat. Yesterday and the day before, we came across ripe mulberries. I'm not sure that I ever had truly sweet, ripe mulberries. They are very tasty.

Mowed Path!

At 2 p.m., under the scorching heat of the sun and with two and a half miles farther to walk on open roads, Beth runs out of water. A lady is resting on her porch and cheerfully provides the ice cold trail magic Beth needs.

We talk with her about our walk, and she tells us she has seen groups of people walking the trail. Perhaps they are section hikers who periodically hike through this area.

Shortly before we reach today's destination, the trail passes a monument and plaque about Fort Brown. The fort was built in 1812 by Colonel Brown. Together with Fort Jennings and Fort Amanda to the south and Fort Winchester to the north, this fort guarded the army supply route into the Maumee Valley. In 1813, General Greene Clay's Kentucky militia, who formed the left wing of Harrison's Army, passed this site in boats, on their way to relieve besieged Fort Meigs.

Flat Roads of Northwest Ohio

An organic farm called "Nothing but Nature" is our destination, and the hosts, Phil and Diane Sherry, greet us. The Sherrys began practicing organic farming 23 years ago when they quit their three-piece-suit jobs. They started small; but as they generated excess produce, they began to sell to the public. They have always used organic practices because "it's the right thing to do for the earth, our health, and the health of the animals." Phil tests the soil and goes to great lengths to make sure the plants are in good soil. In 2002, they became involved in a program for finding workers, World-Wide Opportunities on Organic Farms (WWOOF). The farm provides the workers with hands-on experience for learning about organic farming. They grow a variety of greens, root vegetables, and herbs, as well as raise a few steers, goats, and pigs. They also share work with neighbors for raw honey, melons, cheeses, squash, pumpkins, apples, and pears. Their produce goes to a restaurant in Toledo and a local farm market.

Phil and Diane have an empty, basic cabin with a bed but no running water. We gratefully accept the indoor accommodations. In addition, they invite us to dine with them. Diane prepares a delicious dish of Swiss chard cooked with pineapple and chia seeds. The meal also includes tomatoes, home-baked bread, and meat from their farm. It is a pleasant evening, satiating our appetite while sitting on their weathered deck and chatting about how their place came to be.

Day 61: June 21, Tuesday

Today we successfully rise early, at 4:45 a.m., and are on the road-trail by 5:30. The morning is calm and cool, a mist lies low over fields, and the sky is clear. The moon hangs on the western horizon, and the sun is rising in the east as a yellow-orange ball, promising to later melt us in our tracks.

Within a couple of miles, our road walk turns off onto the canal towpath. The trail has been mowed, and it's an easy walk. At one point, the trail skirts a farmer's field, and we see a raccoon working the grassy edge, moving in the same direction we are. For about 50 paces, the raccoon is not aware of our presence. Finally, it picks up on a sound, looks at us, and then darts into the grass and trees.

We have not been bothered by mosquitoes, as we expected along the old canal waterways and numerous drainage ditches in this flat farmland. One person mentioned that it has been very dry in northwestern Ohio and this has kept the mosquito population down. The fields testify to the dryness; the clay soil we walk across is deeply cracked, and the short stalks of corn are struggling to survive.

My morning snacks consist of a protein bar, Snickers, and Little Debbie donuts. Now doesn't that make you want to long-distance hike? How else can you eat like that and not put on weight?

Crossing from the Delphos Section into the Defiance Section is like driving on a road that crosses a county line, where you leave pavement and then go onto a gravel road. As we enter the Defiance Section, we walk on an off-road stretch that has not been mowed in quite some time, and we must dance around the abundant poison ivy. More frequent mowing would be appreciated.

Fence Crossing

We see our first milkweed blossom today. Milkweeds (family Asclepiadaceae) have been in decline as a result of extensive use of herbicides and changing land use; the plant was historically common and widespread on prairies, but habitat destruction has reduced its range and numbers.

The plant is essential to the survival of the Monarch butterfly, which is now also in rapid decline. Monarch larvae appear to feed exclusively on milkweed. Most milkweed species are toxic to vertebrate herbivores, if ingested. However, the Monarch larvae are unaffected, and after ingesting these toxins, they become toxic themselves to potential predators, or at least, they leave a bitter taste in the mouth.

Monarch butterflies spend winters in Mexico. In February and March, that generation comes out of hibernation to find a mate and then migrate north and east. During migration, they find milkweeds on which to lay their eggs in March or April.

Those eggs begin the first generation of the new year, hatching into larvae in about four days. The larvae feed on the milkweed and are fully grown after about two weeks, when each attaches itself to a stem and transforms into a chrysalis. Ten days later, a butterfly emerges. That butterfly has only two to six weeks to fly farther north before laying eggs to begin the second generation. That generation is born in May and June and the third generation is born in July and August. The fourth generation, born in September and October, is different from the first three generations in that it goes through all the stages but does not die after two to six weeks. Instead, those butterflies migrate from as far away as Canada back to Mexico, where they will live for six to eight months.

The milkweed plant is vital for this life cycle, so if your home is in the Monarchs' flight path, ask a nursery about planting milkweeds for these travelers.

Along the trail, a historical marker and signpost is the only visible evidence that we are at the junction of the Miami and Erie Canal and the Wabash and Erie Canal. The marker reads as follows:

> On this site, the Miami and Erie Canal, that came north from Cincinnati and the Ohio River, intersected with the Wabash and Erie Canal that came from Fort Wayne and Evansville, Indiana. From this point, which became the town of Junction, the canals proceeded as one to Defiance, Toledo, and Lake Erie. From the 1830s to the 1870s, the canals played a key role in the settling of Paulding County, an area that was once part of the Great Black Swamp. They held the promise of easier and quicker passenger transportation and commodity shipping and Junction became a landmark for fugitive slaves escaping to Canada. Once a thriving and growing community, the village of Junction became a forgotten historical note with the passing of the canal era and the coming of the railroads.

Sign at Junction of Canals

We enter the city of Defiance (population 16,836), where the trail goes by a Chief grocery store. We relish the coolness of the store while we buy the usual snacks for the trail and also crab meat salad and freshly cut fruit salad.

The motel is a couple of miles off the trail, so we call a cab and take the easy way.

We have the afternoon to relax, but looking at our schedule, we see that we have several B&B and motel reservations to make for the next week. Scouring the Internet, we are surprised that some accommodations are already booked full, so we lock in reservations where there is availability—which means, of course, that our hiking distances for each day are now fixed.

Journal and section notes completed, we retire for the day.

Chapter 9

EASTWARD BOUND

Day 62: June 22, Wednesday
With every step, we will now be heading east toward our starting point, Headlands Beach, and the completion of our BT Big Loop hike.

Our day begins at 5 a.m. with packing, enjoying the motel's continental breakfast, and calling a cab for a ride back to the trail. We have been warned of severe storms approaching this evening. Fortunately, we expect to arrive at the next motel well before then.

We have about 4 miles of road walk and then 16 miles of off-road trail to cover today. Off-road trail sections are generally met with trepidation because our experience brings visions of fighting through the bushes or dancing around poison ivy. However, we are pleasantly surprised today to find this trail is used both for hiking and biking and is well maintained.

The initial "off-road" section is actually on a 2.7-mile park road. We pass Independence Dam on the Maumee River, a reservoir built to provide water for the canal. It derived its name from a town one mile upstream that grew up during the canal construction. Independence became a thriving community, rivaling Defiance at one time; but, like many canal "boom" towns, the town disappeared when the canal was abandoned.

Following the Maumee River downstream, we find a historic marker along the park road that describes an army camp located here during the winter of the War of 1812. In a diary entry, a private in the regiment referred to the camp as "Fort Starvation."

> Camp No. 3 was located about six miles below Fort Winchester on the north side of the Maumee River. Militiamen from Kentucky, part of the forces led by War of 1812 Brig. Gen. James Winchester, occupied the camp from November 1812 until December 30, 1812. They had marched off to war in summer wearing their linen clothing; unaware they would end up in the heart of the Black Swamp in mid-winter.

With only small huts for shelter, the soldiers endured intense suffering. Canal workers building the Miami and Erie Canal unearthed burial grounds, where it's estimated at least 300 soldiers were buried.

The last 0.7 mile of the nearly three-mile linear park is apparently no longer maintained. The park road is blocked off to motorized vehicles, though shelters and picnic tables are still there. It is a delightful walk among large trees, along the old paved road. Long and narrow, the park at times may be less than 400 yards wide and is bordered on the north by the Miami and Erie Canal and on the south by the Maumee River. When the park road ends, the trail continues onto a dirt track that is mowed at least six feet wide and used by both hikers and bicyclists. We are so pleased to have a true trail that allows us to relax and move along at a steady pace.

On this lovely trail, the first person we meet is a young lady out for a jog with her two dogs. As we meet, we simultaneously say, "Good—somebody has broken the spider webs ahead of me!"

The second person we encounter is an older gentleman out for a two-mile walk. We meet him just before the small town of Florida (population 232). I jokingly say that the town should have a retirement community so that a person can say they retired to Florida. He laughs and says, "You won't believe the number of people who come to the town after a snowstorm and take their picture by the town sign."

Three or four miles down the trail are a couple of mulberry trees with low-hanging branches loaded with berries. We are elated with this savory bounty and spend at least 10 minutes picking and eating berries. Surgical gloves would be handy—the juice is easily squeezed out of the berry when picked, and it dyes our hands and mouths a beautiful, dark reddish-purple.

At Ritter Park in the town of Napoleon (population 8,700), a lady is walking her two small dogs and waves and calls out a greeting. She is very enthusiastic and wants to know what we are doing. After we explain our hike, she asks if she can notify their local newspaper. We tell her we will be at the Best Western tonight, if somebody wishes to contact us.

We bid the lady goodbye, and within a hundred yards we meet Mr. Otto, riding a bicycle. He is a Buckeye Trail maintainer! Thank you, Mr. Otto!

Along the trail, a plaque tells the interesting story of how the town "kept" its name.

> Napoleon was founded in 1834 but its name was almost changed to Henry in 1853. At that time, there was a popular movement to Americanize place names and some citizens of Napoleon wanted to rename it after patriot Patrick Henry. Village Commissioners approved the change in March 1853. In 5 issues printed that autumn, the publisher of the Napoleon *North West* newspaper listed its location as Henry, Ohio. Frenchman Augustin Pilliod, who was starting construction of his three-story flouring mill on Front Street, opposed the measure. On October 10, 1853, the day a mayor and councilmen were to be elected for the newly-incorporated Village of Henry, Pilliod and other opponents staged a demonstration, which blocked both the election and the name change. The village of Napoleon was finally incorporated in 1863.

Towpath Hike-Bike Trail

The Best Western is 0.3 mile north of the trail and next to a travel service center. The motel staff greets us warmly and with more interest in our hike than most people we have met. The people of Napoleon are very welcoming.

We tell the front desk clerk that someone from the newspaper may be in touch, then shower, put on clean clothes, and walk to the travel center restaurant for a mid-afternoon meal. While we are at the restaurant, the hotel lady walks over with a message and phone number to call the local newspaper. When we make the call, we agree to a four-o'clock interview in the hotel lobby.

The interview covers standard questions—the length of the hike, time on the trail, Ohio historical facts along the trail, the different landscapes, information collected for a BT databook, difficulties, and people met—and lasts perhaps 15 minutes. Beth points out the one thing that we have become keenly aware of: On other more popular trails we become immersed in a community of hikers, and conversations center around water sources, trail conditions ahead, campsites, and such topics. On this hike, we have not met anyone who is out for more than an hour or two, and our experiences meeting other people are totally different.

Day 63: June 23, Thursday

Today marks our ninth week on the trail, and our morning routine is: Up at 5 a.m., pack, motel continental breakfast (which is excellent), and hike back to the trail by 6:30.

The local news station reports that the area received about 2.5 inches of rain last night, with some areas getting as much as 3.5 inches. I figure the moisture will bring out the mosquitoes.

The soil must have been very dry prior to the rain; there are only a few standing puddles, and we do not have to slog through any excessive mud. The morning remains overcast, cool, and humid. And indeed, there are pockets along the trail where the mosquitoes seem to have congregated and are waiting for us. But overall, we hike along the trail without any major problems.

With little to distract us along the trail, we reminisce about Beth's friends Art and Tish, who are currently in Eureka, California. Beth had met Tish when she worked in Puerto Rico 30 years ago. They became fast friends and have stayed in touch. Tish's husband, Art, is in the Coast Guard, and she met Art when he was stationed in Puerto Rico over 10 years ago. Tish was a hairdresser and Beth greatly respected her skill. While we were planning our wedding, Beth sought out several hairdressers, attempting to find one that could produce the hairstyle she wished for the wedding, but none of the styles were satisfactory. When Beth found out that Tish would be able to attend our ceremony, she was ecstatic—she knew she would have the hairstyle she wanted.

Providence Dam

Near Grand Rapids, our final destination today, we pass Providence Dam, named after the town of Providence, which was once located across the river from Grand Rapids. The town was born, thrived, and died with the Miami and Erie Canal. Platted in 1835 by French trader Peter Manor, swept by fire in 1846, and ravaged by cholera in 1854, the life of the small town drained away as the canal also declined. Only the Irish canal workers' St. Patrick's Church and Peter Manor's house remain. The Providence Dam was built in 1838 to create a water supply for the canal's remaining 25 miles to Toledo. Peter Manor's Mill stands downstream a half mile, at Lock 9. It operates today as the Isaac Ludwig Historic Mill.

Near the Ludwig Mill, we purchase tickets to experience the Miami and Erie aboard the *Volunteer,* an operating canal boat. We wait in the staging area, where a volunteer dressed in period clothing of 1876 reviews boat safety, gives a brief history of the canal, and sings a canal song while strumming an instrument. With 28 other people, we enjoy a leisurely one-hour ride on the canal. Another costumed volunteer narrates our trip, imagining that we are embarking on a six-day journey to Cincinnati in the year 1876. Four more volunteers act as helmsman, mule guide, and deckhands. You see the reason for the name of this boat.

Canal Boat *Volunteer*

The boat glides along silently; there are no bumps, jostling, or sounds of engines. This ride gives us the added pleasure of going through Lock 9. The boat enters the lock, and the lower gates close. As water fills the lock, the boat rises four feet. Then the upper gates are opened and the boat proceeds. A quarter mile farther up the canal, the boat is turned around and we go back through Lock 9 in the opposite direction. The narrator—still in character—politely explains that a certain crewmember (who will be chastised!) has forgotten to load a cargo of bricks and we must return to remedy the situation.

After the canal boat ride, we cross the Maumee River on the State Route 295 bridge and enter Grand Rapids (population 986).

The Grand Rapids area was a rich hunting ground for many native Indian tribes. As settlers moved west, hostilities arose. President Washington appointed General Anthony Wayne to lead forces into the area. After building Fort Defiance in 1794, at the junction of the Maumee and Auglaize River, Wayne advanced down the Maumee Valley. At the famous Battle of Fallen Timbers, Wayne's troops defeated the Indian warriors commanded by Blue Jacket. This battle resulted in the Treaty of Greenville of 1794.

We are in the Great Black Swamp of Ohio. The formation of this large wetland goes back to the Ice Age, when northwestern Ohio was covered by a massive ice sheet. When the ice melted, the area from Fort Wayne, Indiana, to western New York was covered by a large lake (named Lake Maumee by geologists). After water eventually drained away, swamps formed in the lowlands. The Great Black Swamp, 120 miles long and 30 to 40 miles wide, included the Maumee Valley. The heavily wooded swamp was a barrier to westward settlement. However, by 1900, through the use of a major system of dikes and ditches, the area was drained, and the dark soils of the old swamp became fertile agricultural lands.

We have a reservation at the Mill House Bed and Breakfast, originally a steam-powered mill, built around 1900. Farmers with horse-drawn wagons brought their grain here to have it reduced to flour or livestock feed. We are staying in a room named after the first white settler in Grand Rapids, Edward Howard.

Our early dinner is next door at Pisanello's, where we enjoy the salad bar and whatever pizza creation we want. The restaurant has the unique procedure of leaving your ordered pizza in the warming tray at the counter, and you eat as much or as little as you want of your pizza plus whatever you might like of what has been left by other customers.

While we're enjoying pizza, our hosts at the B&B, Ron and Kathy, kindly do our laundry!

Day 64: June 24, Friday

We set out at 5:45 a.m. Our clothes are clean, and we've had a delightful breakfast. Last night, our hosts put a veggie quiche and a bowl of cut fruit in the fridge for us to enjoy this morning.

The day begins at 60 degrees, which is cooler than we have had for a while. As the sun rises, its light paints the clouds—first magenta and then a bright orange—before burning the clouds off and leaving the day in full sun with light winds.

The towpath today is crushed limestone; it makes walking easy and allows us to enjoy our surroundings. The area is remote enough that bird songs are once again quite noticeable.

After about a mile, the canal to our left is no longer full of water; rather, it is dry at some places or, at others, filled with shallow water that is covered with green duckweed. A number of fallen trees are also lying across the channel.

On our right, the Maumee River is quite wide, perhaps 800 to 1,000 feet. The current is surprisingly swift for such a flat area.

The only issue we have this morning is the abundance of spider webs across the trail. They are just single, delicate strands, but they cling and accumulate, so I have to constantly brush them off. At 7 a.m., we see a park vehicle driving toward us, and our greeting to him includes our thanks for breaking the webs ahead of us.

Towpath

After 5.8 miles, we arrive at Bend View Park. The Maumee River makes a 90-degree turn, creating a panoramic view of the expansive river. Just past this area, an eagle rises from the trees and soars across the river.

About an hour later, we arrive in Waterville, at the place where a massive limestone rock, crowned by trees and low brush, rises in the center of the Maumee River. This rock and the settlement that once existed here on the banks of the river are known as Roche de Boeuf (or Roche de Bout).

The large outcropping was a sacred meeting site of the Native Americans and the place where they gathered before the Battle of Fallen Timbers in August 1794. In the early 1900s, the Lima-Toledo Traction Company built the Interurban Bridge to carry their electric railway over the Maumee and placed one bridge support on the island. About one-third of the rock was blasted away in that construction, an event that caused consternation for many. Once the world's longest earthen-filled, reinforced concrete bridge, it is no longer in use. The

Lima-Toledo company closed down the commuter railway in 1937, but Roche de Boeuf remains a celebrated landmark in this area.

Roche de Boeuf

Bonanza! While enjoying our pleasant walk into Waterville (population 5,509), with the day still cool and the shadows long in the morning sun, Beth finds a crisp one-dollar bill. With the eight cents found over the past couple of weeks the "homeless couple" will end their trip with change to spare!

Whether new or old, the Waterville homes along the river have been treated with care, and their beauty is enhanced by neatly tended landscaping. The town itself has a quaint, two-block area that includes an inviting sidewalk café at Dale's Diner. But it is still early, and we leave town on the State Route 65 bridge over the Maumee River.

Our reservation tonight is at the Days Inn in Bowling Green. The Buckeye Trail does not go into the city of Bowling Green, so when we see a car repair shop with the big doors open, we inquire within if anyone knows how we can find a ride into town to the motel. The owner says he is about ready to go into town, he offers us a ride, and he even goes out of his way to drop us off at the motel entrance.

A Bob Evans restaurant is next door, and since neither of us has ever eaten a dinner at Bob Evans, that is where we head. Beth has a fish dinner, and I select a chicken dinner; both are good and satisfy our appetite for the evening.

The end of our thru-hike is approaching, and we use the evening to plan out our next several nights and to write journal and BT section notes. The motel has business cards for two cab companies. Beth calls each one and schedules a morning ride with the company that seems to be the most pleasant to deal with. One company seemed a bit aloof—and not one we could count on for an early-morning ride!

Day 65: June 25, Saturday

Our morning again starts early, and the continental breakfast at the motel is not fully set out. However, the cold cereal, yogurt, and toast provide sufficient calories to begin the day.

Our cab is punctual, arriving at 6 a.m., and we begin hiking in the first rays of sunlight.

The sun is briefly a sliver on the horizon, but it grows to a reddish-orange, sweltering ball that will soon make us take shelter under our umbrellas. Here the farmers have not left many fence rows or lined the roads with trees, so we do not have even the brief relief of long morning shadows.

Our Buckeye Trail thru-hike will soon be finished, and as we walk, our thoughts drift back to the first long-distance hike we did together in 2013.

We had been working on home projects, planting flowers, splitting flower bulbs, and doing a little canoeing, kayaking, and bicycling. We biked to be outdoors and also to condition our legs—the thought had been growing that in late August we would hike the John Muir Trail though the High Sierra of California.

This 210-mile trail follows the Sierra Nevada mountain range from Yosemite National Park to its southern terminus at Mount

Whitney. In 2009, my sister, Joanne, and I had hiked a loop of the trail from Kings Canyon up to Rae Lakes on the John Muir Trail. Ever since this small taste of the High Sierra, I had been dreaming of hiking the entire JMT.

At the Buckeye TrailFest, Beth and I had attended a presentation on the John Muir Trail, and Beth was immediately eager to hike it. My own experience made me feel she would love hiking through those mountains. So we purchased hiking equipment for her, tested it on a weekend hike with a local club, and began making plans for California and the High Sierra.

As we walk the Buckeye Trail today, the first town we encounter is Pemberville (population 1,403), a quaint town on the Portage River. It has a couple of diners, a Sunoco station, an IGA, and an opera house that was built in 1892 at the height of the region's oil boom. Apparently, such a facility in the older days also included the town jail, fire department, and council chambers. The building gradually fell into disrepair, but in 1999 was restored to its original grandeur. The opera house is not open this early in the morning, and we must view only its beautiful, red-brick exterior.

Cooling off in Garden Sprinklers

On the roads outside of Pemberville, bicyclists begin to pass us in groups of 2 to 20. Evidently, this is the weekend of a multiple sclerosis fund-raising bicycle ride to Sandusky Bay. The riders were given the choice of cycling a distance of 50, 75, or 100 miles. How lamentable that one of their food stops is not along the BT. We may have been offered a share of a good meal or enjoyed a relaxing rest stop, exchanging stories about our respective adventures. Both possibilities would have been trail magic!

In Elmore (population 1,404), we pick up the North Coast Inland Trail at the town park. We pause for a rest and to call a cab that will pick us up in Lindsey and transport us to our motel in Fremont tonight, another Days Inn. Even though Lindsey is six miles away, I can tell the cab company with confidence that we will meet the cab in 2.5 hours. Northwest Ohio farmland is incredibly flat and unbroken for as far as the eye can see, and our hiking pace is the same regardless of whether we are on a road or bikeway.

In Lindsey (population 437), we meet up with the bicyclists again at one of their food stops. We are not offered and do not partake of their food—but some fresh fruit would have been very tasty.

Anyway, this is the end of our exertion today. I pause long enough to speak with one of the volunteers about our walk on the Buckeye Trail, and she mentions that her son may want to hike the BT.

We head to the Village Market for ice cream and something to drink and then sit on a shaded bench, waiting for our ride.

When I made the reservation at the Fremont Days Inn, I failed to inquire whether restaurants were nearby. Fortunately, the motel has its own restaurant, and we can walk down the hallway for dinner.

I had hoped to stay at a B&B on the Buckeye Trail in downtown Fremont, to be in close proximity to the President Hayes Memorial. However, that B&B is permanently closed; and, regrettably, all the motels are five miles north of town.

EASTWARD BOUND

Day 66: June 26, Sunday

We enjoy the opportunity to rest a while longer and not get up until the late hour of 5:45 a.m. There are not many hiking preparations that must be done today—from Lindsey, we'll be slackpacking back to Fremont and the Hayes Presidential Museum and then be back here for another night at the Days Inn. The motel has a good continental breakfast, and we linger over it until the cab arrives at 7 a.m. to transport us back to the Buckeye Trail in Lindsey.

⬥ ⬥

A leisurely morning allows our conversation to go back to the John Muir Trail once again.

Ready for the JMT hike, Beth and I flew out to San Francisco. Jason (Joanne's son), his wife, Alicia, and Beth's friend Tish met us at the airport and brought us to Jason and Alicia's home for dinner. Tish joined us, and then drove us to her home for the night.

The next morning, Tish and her husband, Art, drove us to Yosemite National Park for the start of our much anticipated, 17-day hike on the John Muir Trail.

We were fortunate to be granted walk-in permits for hiking the trail and also to hike up Half Dome. Art and Tish joined us for lunch at a park café before they sent us on our way.

The sign at the beginning of our hike indicated we had 211 miles to Mount Whitney. We planned, however, to add miles to the trip by going up Half Dome, climbing to Clouds Rest, and detouring to Lake Edison to resupply. Once we finished the hike and exited Mount Whitney (the southern terminus), logistics involved hitching a ride to the town of Lone Pine, where we would clean up and spend the night. The next day, we would travel by bus to the city of Ridgeway to pick up a rental car to Las Vegas, and then we would fly home from there.

Today's schedule is much less complicated. We carry no equipment burden this morning, and we can walk like a happy couple out for a Sunday stroll in the park. High cirrus clouds mute the intensity of the sun, and the morning is idyllic. Trees line the bikeway, and a light breeze rustles the leaves. Mosquitoes do occasionally make their presence known—it is never Camelot on the trail.

We meet a bicyclist resting alongside the trail. He has a bike trailer in tow, so I ask him where he is traveling from and going to. This is only his second day out, but his intention is to bicycle around Lake Erie. He has already completed a ride around Lake Michigan and Lake Ontario, with hopes of completing a circuit around each of the Great Lakes. What a great idea for bicycle rides!

We arrive in Fremont and walk to AM Korner Café for an early lunch, though the *AM* stands for *morning* and breakfast items are their specialty. Afterward, we walk to the Hayes Presidential Memorial and have time to wander around the grounds before our scheduled 12:30 p.m. tour of the home. The grounds are mowed on the 25-acre estate and have many large trees, creating a beautiful, park-like setting. The estate is named Spiegel Grove because the pools of water that collected after a rain reflected the towering trees like mirrors. *Spiegel* is the German word for *mirror*.

Rutherford B. Hayes Home

The two-and-a-half-story, brick Victorian home has 23,000 square feet with 31 rooms. When it was donated to the state in 1965, five generations had lived in the home. Nearly all the original furniture from the 1800s is still in the house, and it is really quite impressive to tour a home that is in essentially the same condition as it was at the time it was built. It is easy to imagine the family moving around in daily activities or having a grand party. The State of Ohio restored the house to its original décor, taking guidance from historical photos and working through layers of paint or wallpaper.

Rutherford B. Hayes was born on October 4, 1822, in Delaware, Ohio. He graduated from Kenyon College in 1842 and Harvard Law School in 1845 and practiced law in Lower Sandusky before moving to Cincinnati in December 1849. Opposing the expansion of slavery, he joined the Republican Party in the 1850s and played an increasingly important role in city politics. In 1852, he married Lucy Ware Webb, who would later become the first woman with a college degree to step into the role of First Lady of the United States. They had seven sons and one daughter. Hayes took a seat in the House of Representatives and later resigned to run for governor of Ohio. He is the first Ohio governor to serve three terms (from 1868 to 1877). He moved to his Spiegel Grove estate during his term as governor, and in 1876, he ran for United States President against Democrat Samuel J. Tilden, the governor of New York.

It was a bitterly contested election—Tilden won the popular vote but lacked one electoral vote for victory. The outcome depended upon contested electoral votes in three southern states: Louisiana, South Carolina, and Florida. Hayes needed all three to win. A congressional committee was formed to settle the matter. The decision went to Rutherford B. Hayes, who became the 19th president, serving from 1877 to 1881. He supported Civil Service reform and hard money policies, and worked to reconcile the North and the South by ending reconstruction and withdrawing federal troops from South Carolina and Louisiana. President Hayes and First Lady Lucy Webb are buried on the Spiegel Grove estate.

The Rutherford B. Hayes Presidential Library and Museum is America's first presidential library and is celebrating its centennial this year (2016).

Our time at Spiegel Grove and the museum comes to an end, and we call a cab and retire again to the Days Inn in north Fremont.

Day 67: June 27, Monday

After a continental breakfast at the motel and a 10-minute cab ride to the Buckeye Trail, by 6:10 a.m. we are heading out of Fremont, once again on the paved North Coast Inland Trail.

The easy bike path allows us to continue comparing this BT experience with our John Muir Trail hike.

The first day on the JMT was only a four-mile hike to our Little Yosemite campsite. The second day we had planned to hike up Half Dome, so we were up early and even walked the first 30 minutes with headlamps. This was the beginning our first major hike together. I had seen the High Sierra before and was looking forward to the entire adventure; Beth was glad to be outdoors and backpacking. Mention any adventure "outdoors," and Beth is *in!*

But when we reached the base of Half Dome and she saw the cabled, 70-degree slope up to the granite monolith, she thought, *What are you doing here? Do you really want to do this?*

A father and his 10-year-old daughter began the ascent, and with that example before us, we, too, began the climb.

At the top, we enjoyed our reward—a vast, panoramic view of the Yosemite Valley. It was a fitting preview. Every day on the JMT provided stunning vistas that have few equals anywhere in the world, and I was thrilled to have Beth along to share the sights and experiences with me.

✥ ✥

This morning on the BT is nearly a repeat of yesterday—except that we will be hiking twice as far and the temperature is expected to rise to 94 degrees. It is much hotter and more humid hiking in Ohio during the summer than in the cooler, drier altitude we experienced on our hikes out west. We have also discovered that this Ohio heat will melt any chocolate in protein bars or candies! It's better to have crackers, peanuts, sunflower seeds, or protein bars without chocolate.

The JMT had no chain motels along the trail, but there were many campsites to choose from. As we hiked the BT over these past couple of hot, humid weeks, we often looked forward to hotels and B&Bs with air conditioning, but both of us missed the tent-camping experience. When we are hiking a trail, it seems more appropriate to spend the nights outside. However, we've found that campsites along the Buckeye Trail where one can wash and/or obtain water from a clear flowing stream are scare or nonexistent. A second option is camping in established state park or private campgrounds, and the third option is staying at the motels, lodges, and B&Bs.

We will say that our B&B experiences have proven to be an exception to our preference to be camping. The bed and breakfasts are special in many ways, and the hosts are generally pleasant to meet and full of local information. Planning this hike, I intentionally searched for B&Bs along the route. Every one of our stays at such establishments has been an extraordinary experience.

Our first stop this morning is in the town of Clyde (population 6,300). It is 8:50 a.m., and the Family Dollar store does not open until 9:00, so, instead, we walk across the street to a gas station food mart to use the restroom and ATM and to buy snack food for two days. We're on the trail again in 20 minutes.

Upon reaching the outskirts of Bellevue (population 8,076), we find that the North Coast Inland Trail, which the BT has been following, has not been completed through this town. The paved path becomes a gravel road along the railroad tracks and then turns onto a road south and by-passes Bellevue's town center. We, however, want to be on Main Street, where our destination, the Victorian Tudor Inn B&B, is located. Once again, we're thankful for the convenience of our smartphones; we click on Google Maps and find our best walking route to the inn.

Serendipitously, a Wendy's restaurant is located three buildings away from the inn, and we stop in for a salad lunch. Yesterday, it was pleasant to be inside a museum during the hot, humid afternoon. Today, it is pleasant—and a relief—to have completed the 15-mile hike to Bellevue by 11:30 a.m.

Our B&B host, Richard, accommodates our early arrival. Richard was a political science professor before becoming a dean at universities in Delaware, Massachusetts, Rhode Island, Pennsylvania, and Wyoming. As beautiful as Wyoming is, it only took one winter there for him to decide it was time to retire and return to his roots in Bellevue, where he has family. It took him a few months to find the house he really wanted, a beautiful, 1906, eight-bedroom Victorian Tudor. His home is packed with antiques he has collected over many years, and he has enjoyed operating the Tudor as a B&B for the past eight years.

For a "picnic" dinner we go to the Bassett grocery store for mac & cheese, couscous salad, baked beans, Bing cherries and watermelon. Back at the house, we sit on the spacious, shaded front porch and enjoy dinner and the summer breeze. The setting transports us back in time one hundred years, when the home was much newer, and we can envision neighbors ambling by.

Our host and his neighbor and boyhood friend, David, regale us with stories of the town, the B&B's patrons, and past owners of the house. When Richard asks where we are staying tomorrow night and we tell him we've made a reservation at the Victorian Lady B&B in Norwalk, his face lights up and he declares we have chosen the best place to stay in that town. Apparently, the Victorian Lady is in the heart of Norwalk's historic district and the street is lined with beautiful old homes. We have that to look forward to.

EASTWARD BOUND

Day 68, June 28, Tuesday

Up at 5 a.m. and packed, we look in the kitchen for breakfast. We had mentioned we would be up earlier to benefit from the cooler morning temperatures for hiking, so Richard promised to have breakfast items out. We find a small bowl of fresh fruit, toasted bagels with cream cheese and jam, and a couple of cookies to satisfy our morning appetite.

We are out the door and on the trail by 6:00, and the temperature is already at 65 degrees. The sun rises with every intention of making its presence felt.

Since the North Coast Inland Trail is not completed through Bellevue, our walk starts off on sidewalks until we reach the bike path on the outskirts at the other end of town at 6:45 a.m. Here, the path is crushed limestone, which makes for comfortable walking. Long shadows stretch across the flat corn and soybean fields. The train tracks to our left are very active lines, and several trains pass us during the morning. Whistles blow and diesel fumes briefly envelope us as each train rumbles by.

Morning Farm Scene

One pleasure of hiking with Beth is learning what she enjoys seeing. What captures her imagination? Occasionally, it is simply good to have her jog me out of my thoughts, when she points out something of interest or a spectacular view that I may have walked by. And just to prove the point, Beth spots a fox as it dashes behind a clump of trees; I, of course, miss the scene. We both see the hawk that soars low overhead, screeching, perhaps in search of its morning breakfast or just annoyed at having been disturbed by a couple of backpackers. We have seen hawks along nearly every section of the Buckeye Trail.

Hiking on the bike path, we keep a three-mile-per-hour pace and arrive at the Victorian Lady B&B at 10:15 a.m. Our host, Vickie, is here to greet us. We had let her know we would be coming in early, and her schedule has allowed her to be here.

Vickie quickly shows us around the house and to "Biltmore," our room for the night. Throughout the house hang many pictures of Victorian ladies in various settings. The three-story house was built in 1890 and is 7,000 square feet. Vickie and her husband, Tim Dauch, purchased the property in 2001, after it had sat empty for several months. They renovated it and began the B&B business in 2005, and she enjoys meeting the variety of people who arrive as her guests.

A notebook with information for guests includes a page outlining the history of the home:

> The Queen Anne mansion was built for W.W. Graham in 1890. Mr. Graham came to Ohio from Illinois in 1880. He was a paymaster and railroad bridge contractor for the Wheeling & Lake Erie Railroad. He constructed and built nearly all the bridges and furnished the bulk of all the ties for the Wheeling & Lake Erie Railroad. His contracting reached the large sum of one and one-half million dollars. He also built more than seventy miles of bridges for the Baltimore & Ohio Railroad. Mr. Graham married Nellie M. Griggs in 1864 in Illinois.

Her father was the general contractor for the Wheeling & Lake Erie Railroad. They had two children, Maude and King. Nellie passed away in 1887. In 1890 Mr. Graham married Carrie M. Rude of Sandusky. They bought the land on West Main Street from John and Frances Gardiner and began building their home. W.W. Graham passed away in 1915. The house was sold at an estate auction for $6,700. Since then it has been owned by 7 other families.

My hike today is not over. I want to advance down the trail and use a taxi to return to the Victorian Lady. This has two advantages: 1) I can hike some trail miles without a backpack and 2) it puts Findley Lake campground within easy hiking distance for tomorrow. Beth will take the opportunity to enjoy a leisurely afternoon at the B&B.

As I set off, it is now mostly cloudy and the temperature remains cool, a good day to do the miles. The trail goes through downtown Norwalk and exits the east side on sidewalks and suburban roads.

After a few miles, the BT reconnects with the North Coast Inland Trail. This path is similar to what we walked on this morning, with gravel and crushed limestone. The hike is rather uneventful; there are no facilities along the way, and I miss sharing these miles with my hiking partner. I do see another hawk and several chipmunks. Deerflies occasionally accompany me and keep me moving.

I had planned to hike to the end of the bicycle path, and once I arrive there, I call the cab company. It will be an hour and a half before someone can pick me up, so I wait and take the time to work on my journal and databook notes.

Tomorrow we will leave the North Coast Inland Trail, which heads northeast from here to Lorain. We will head southeast, on roads, until we enter Findley Lake State Park and join a footpath.

The stretch of trail we have been on is actually a recently proposed change to the Buckeye Trail. Formalities of the change are still in the works; but as we planned our hike, it was suggested that we explore the proposed change to gather information for the databook. We have certainly enjoyed the proposed route, which offered two delightful overnight accommodations. We did note that during our time on the North Coast Inland Trail over the past few days, no one approached us to ask about our backpacks and where be might be coming from or going to.

Once again back at the Victorian Lady, I take a shower while Beth orders a pizza and salad for us. We use the upstairs foyer to eat, relax, and have a quiet conversation.

Day 69: June 29, Wednesday

Hills! Well if you can call a 10 to 20 foot change in elevation a hill. The terrain now presents some gentle ups and downs. Gone is the pancake-flat farmland that we have hiked through the last couple of weeks. Ditches are shallow, not the six-foot-plus deep scars across the land that drained the Black Swamp to create rich farmland.

Our day began at 5 a.m., with breakfast that consisted of small boxes of cereal, a little fruit, milk, and juice. A cab deposits us at our starting point at 6:25, and we immediately notice the rolling terrain as we look down the road. There are also more wood lots breaking up the farmland and fewer views across expansive fields.

The sun is already up in the blue sky, and this part of Ohio remains very dry.

Within a couple of miles, we cross the Vermilion River. Here the river is a small stream and not yet the beautiful river we have known and canoed beneath high cliffs as it makes its way to Lake Erie.

The Buckeye Trail is on roads until we enter Findley Lake State Park and join a footpath.

At 8:30 a.m., it is still and quiet, with only the chirping of birds and a light summer breeze. Hiking in and out of tree shadows, we feel the alternating warmth of the sun and the coolness of the shade. Beth is always the first to suffer in the heat, and she enjoys the cooler temperature.

A woodpecker catches our attention; it has been some time since we've heard a woodpecker. We also notice dozens of killdeer in the fields, flying and chirping as if to protect their nests—an unusual number of killdeer, I think.

Our walk the last few days toward Findley Lake State Park has been across relatively flat, fertile farmland where millions of bushels of corn, wheat, and soybean are grown. Fields of neat green rows led to distant wood lots, farmhouses, barns, and silos. The waterways ran dirty and muddy, carrying the fine clay and silt particles of a soil rich for growing food.

What a contrast to our walk to the Thousand Island Lake of the High Sierra!

On that hike, we crossed over a pass and were greeted by a stunning vista—a large, clear, blue lake with a "thousand" islands and a backdrop of the towering Rocky Mountains. Streams in the High Sierra run over rock and are clear and cool. The jagged mountains delight the eye with their many different facets that change with every step we take.

Together, Beth and I have now seen and shared the experience of the mountains as well as the landscape of Ohio. They are both visual and emotional feelings that continue to bond us together. The miles we hiked to reach Findley Lake did not come any easier than our hike to Thousand Island Lake. We struggled, persevered, and rejoiced as one.

It is early Wednesday afternoon when we arrive at Findley Lake State Park campground. We have the pick of the campsites and check in, set up our tent, and eat ice cream and a snack.

I take a walk to investigate where the Buckeye Trail footpath exits the park. I hike farther than the one mile where the BT is supposed to diverge from the well-trodden park path and exit the park. In my haste, I must have missed the turn-off. Not wishing to try again, I decide I will have to be more vigilant tomorrow.

We have not heard cicadas since our walk through southern Ohio, but here they are plentiful, and their droning sound is quite noticeable.

We have been told that at their peak this summer, the sound was deafening.

This part of Ohio was home to the Erie Indians long before the first settlers arrived. Decades after the Indians were forcibly removed and the forested lands converted to fields, Guy B. Findley, a Lorain County Common Pleas Judge, purchased tracts of agricultural land in 1936 and 1937 and donated it to the state of Ohio. The Division of Forestry and the Civilian Conservation Corps planted nearly half a million trees on the land. In 1950, the forest was transferred to the Division of Parks and Recreation to be maintained as a state park. An earthen dam, started in 1954 and completed in 1956, created the 93-acre lake. The campground has 90 electric sites and 181 non-electric sites and showers, flush toilets, laundry facilities, and a camp store.

The camp store makes pizza, and that is precisely what we want for dinner. All journal and databook notes are written, and it is now hiker midnight. It has been a while since I made that deadline.

Day 70, June 30, Thursday

We stir at 5:15 a.m., pack, eat a honey bun for breakfast, and Beth has a V8 juice. On the trail, we have belVita crackers, cheese crackers, protein bars (non-chocolate), and trail mix. We pack only cold foods for our meals, but the Buckeye Trail goes through many towns, which allows us to purchase more substantial meals at restaurants. The better campgrounds have also had good restaurants or camp stores.

At 6:00, we are on the trail through the woods of Findley Lake State Park. It is cool again this morning at 53 degrees. We have gotten so used to the hot temperatures that 53 feels almost cold.

Along the trail, Beth spots a small raccoon climbing up a tree.

Just as I mention that there should be a spur trail leading out of the park to a road, we spot a path that looks more like an animal trail. It leads to the road, but there is no BT sign. Since the trail is barely visible, it is little wonder that I missed it in my rush yesterday.

EASTWARD BOUND

Within a tenth of a mile on the road walk, Beth spots another raccoon, and this one is a mother with three young. For me, it is a rare sighting and a treat.

The sky is the showstopper today. At first, the clouds are white paint splattered on a blue background, and the artist has made small sweeps with a brush across the blue, creating thin, wispy extensions to the many little clouds. Later, the clouds grow a little larger, similar to a bright white cumulus cloud, but the artist has again taken the brush and swept broadly to make delicate, feathery streamers from each cloud across the rich blue background. The wind painting the sky mesmerizes us all day.

Again, we see many killdeer. Maybe it's their nesting time. We hear a hawk screeching high in the distance and later have the pleasure of seeing one closer as it flies out of a tree in a wood lot. We are seeing more chipmunks and groundhogs.

At 8:30 a.m., we pass Martin's Blueberry Farm. The temptation of blueberries for breakfast calls us in, but it is a pick-your-own field, and we are not interested in standing and picking blueberries. We had hoped to purchase a pint and eat them as we walked.

We have an off-road section across Spencer Lake Wildlife Area. On the Buckeye Trail map, the description is as follows:

> After 0.3 miles reach parking area just before barricade. Cross barricade onto former road and continue on causeway across Spencer Lake. After 0.3 miles at second barricade, join access road near parking and continue east.

When an "off-road" section is mentioned, we never know just what trail conditions we will encounter. This time, we are amazed to find a concrete sidewalk across the causeway and neatly mowed grass on both sides.

At 9:30 a.m., we hike into Sunset Lake Campground, a private campground around a small lake. The name brings memories, again, of the John Muir Trail. On our second night on the trail, we camped at a "Sunrise Lake." We had the place to ourselves, and we set up our tent right at the water's edge. Beth and I were not on a honeymoon, but many couples would cherish such a setting as we had on that lake in the wilderness. We waded in the cool lake, as we let the water wash off the day's sweat. And what a pleasure it was to share such a place!

We do not stop at Ohio's Sunset Lake. We had considered spending the night here, but since we've arrived so early on a beautiful hiking day, we are compelled to hike on.

The landscape continues to gradually change. We are walking past fewer fields and more residential homes, generally on one or more acres of land.

Finally, we arrive at Lester Rail Trail, part of the Medina County park system. We divert into the community of Mallet Creek, which has a small food mart. After purchasing a couple of drinks and snacks, we relax on a shaded bench for half an hour.

In a couple of miles, the trail ends, and we have a short road walk to State Route 18, where we call a cab. We are whisked seven miles to the Red Roof Inn, glad for a shower after a nearly 25-mile day. Doing more miles today means fewer miles tomorrow, leaving us time to relax with family we are hoping to meet.

We complete our day at one of the earliest Denny's restaurants. The 60s and 70s music and polished chrome steel exterior accompany the standard Denny's fare—but the prices are 2016.

Later, Beth does a load of laundry as I begin to journal.

Yesterday Beth found a penny. Today, I found a penny. We are doing so well that we may have to upgrade our trail completion celebration from bottled water to soda for everyone.

Chapter 10

FAMILY AND HOME

Day 71: July 1, Friday

As I watch the morning rainfall, I think how fortunate it is that today I have only a dozen miles to hike, and it is a slackpack hike through Medina. The rain quickly passes, and I'm able to begin the hike around 10 a.m.

A cab transports me back to begin the hike. Beth is not feeling well and opts to rest, thinking she is perhaps a bit dehydrated.

My hike is on sidewalks into Medina's town center, where a gazebo anchors a one-block-square park.

The trail then leaves the city center on the 0.9-mile paved Champion Creek hike/bike trail.

Without a pack, I feel like I'm floating along. The trail turns onto busy State Route 18, but even when the sidewalk ends, it is pleasant walking—a mowed grassy berm several feet away from the busy road.

Finally, the BT turns onto a path around Lake Medina, following the lake for about one mile, with views of a few beautiful homes on the opposite shore. The hike then gradually exits Medina through the northeastern suburbs, and I leave the trail and walk back to the motel.

Sue and Brad (my sister and my brother-in-law) and my mom arrive at 3:15 p.m. We sit in the motel room, catching up on family news, most of which concerns my dad, who, a few weeks ago, cracked four vertebrae in his neck and now must wear a neck brace. Beth and I are anxious to hear how he is healing and whether he will be able to attend the family reunion at the end of July. Mom is doing some gardening around the villa and walking their little dog, Madel Poo. Sue and Brad have pictures of their grandchildren and laugh as they recount the children's antics.

Restaurant with Brad, Sue, and mother Evelyn Hewett

Brad drives us into downtown Medina to the Main Street Café. From our seats there, we have a pleasant view of the town park across the street. We give an "excellent" rating to the food, the décor, and the ambiance of the restaurant. The menu has a good selection of vegetarian food. Beth has stir-fried veggies over rice, Mom and Brad each have a triple Reuben sandwich, and Sue and I have veggie hummus burritos. Some food is boxed up for takeout because we all want to leave room for Sue's dessert.

Back at the motel, we congregate in the breakfast room, and Sue brings out her black raspberry pie. She makes delicious pies, and this one is no exception. At this point in our hike, we love fruit, and nothing equals fruit in a pie smothered in whipped cream!

Sadly, we have a few things to do before hiker's midnight and must say goodbye. We thank them for driving over and sharing a few hours of our adventure.

We also smile as they leave—they take with them all the weight of our camping gear. Our tent, sleeping bags, mats, and everything we won't need in the last five days of our walk drives off with them. The remainder of our nights will be inside, on soft beds.

Beth and I have loved all of our many hikes; but as each drew to a close, we looked forward to returning to the familiarity of home and family. And so it is with this adventure. It has been a long and challenging walk, but it was also filled with so many wonderful impressions of Ohio.

Beth is feeling her chipper self again and is ready for a day of hiking tomorrow. She even has the energy to dye her hair for the homecoming "parade."

Day 72: July 2, Saturday

We are up at 5 a.m., pack our backpacks, and go to the motel lobby to wait for our ride back to the trail. Some breakfast food is already out, so we grab a quick bite to eat.

Our packs are so much lighter. We recall the last segment of our John Muir Trail hike—quite different than our last days on the BT.

On the JMT, we were required to use bear vaults. One bear vault sufficed—until we reached Edison Lake, where we resupplied with enough food to last us until we reached the southern terminus, Mount Whitney. A second bear vault was necessary then, and Beth carried that (which itself weighed two and a half pounds) and four days of food within the vault, probably 8-10 more pounds. She shouldered the weight without complaint, but she was glad to see each day's worth of food disappear.

This morning, the BT instantly throws us back into a landscape of rock cliffs and ledges. The trail winds between a few tall cliffs and through narrow passages in Hinckley Reservation.

Still reminiscing about our John Muir hike, I recall the areas on that trail with quartzite stones. As we hiked, I scanned the small stones, looking for a special one. When I found one that suited me, I stashed it in my backpack.

Trail through Hinckley Reservation

As the BT crosses Hinckley Reservation, it is a pleasure to walk this well-traveled path through tall and majestic trees. We pass Whipps Ledges picnic area and then a hay field, where a bench provides for a moment of rest, looking out over the field, the trees, and a distant valley. The BT map states that this spot has the inconspicuous distinction of being "perhaps the highest point on the Buckeye Trail, 1,290 feet." Even more wonderful than the view is our find close by—the best black raspberry patch we have encountered. We enjoy a couple handfuls of lusciously delicious berries.

FAMILY AND HOME

It has been a delight to backpack with Beth. She enjoys being outdoors and is always looking out for other people's welfare and socializing with people we meet along the trail. Something special is added to our hike as people relax with us and enjoy getting to know us. Beth deserves the credit for this; people can easily relate to her and soon feel comfortable calling her a friend. She certainly has become *my* best friend.

⸸ ⸸

Today has been cool (72 degrees) and overcast. Our two bottles of water easily get us through today's hike, with plenty to spare. Our milestone today is crossing over I-77; we are once again on the east side of that interstate. It has been many weeks and adventures ago that we crossed to the west side, north of Marietta.

There seems to be more excitement in the air as the roads and landscape begin to look more familiar and we begin reconnecting with family. Today, it is Beth's family who meet up with us. Her sister Susan meets us at the Bedford Section trailhead and drives us to her house. We have lunch with Susan and her sons, daughters, sons-in-law, and grandchildren. Enough of her family is visiting to fill the bedrooms, and so she takes us to her brother Michael's house for dinner and the night. Dinner is a feast of smoked chicken and ribs, grilled salmon, potatoes with cheese, baked beans, macaroni salad, watermelon, cheesecake and ice cream. Beth's parents drive over to join us, too, and Beth has a delightful time catching up with everybody's jobs and activities.

Day 73: July 3, Sunday

We learn that the Quality Inn, our intended destination today, had a fire in the laundry room and the motel is closed for a few weeks. We will have to hike farther than planned, to the Hampton Inn in Solon.

We are up at 5:30 and eat a breakfast of cold cereal and toast. At 6:30, just as Michael prepares to drive us up to the trail, Beth notices hawks on a pine tree branch low to the ground in Michael's backyard. They must be yearling red-tailed hawks.

The start of the Bedford Section is a triple trail junction (the Medina, Akron, and Bedford sections meet here). We ended the Medina section at the junction yesterday, started here last fall to hike the Akron Section heading south, and today we turn northeast into the Bedford Section. Michael takes our picture by the BT sign along Valley Parkway before we say, "Happy trails. See you again soon."

Beth with brother Michael

Our hike begins in a wooded stretch; the trees are a good size, and the forest feels open rather than closed in. The trail is well used and easy to walk. It is a pleasant, cool morning to hike

Emerging from the woods, we cross the Chippewa River and then the Cuyahoga Valley Scenic Railroad tracks. A wrought iron bridge crosses the Cuyahoga River. Built in 1881, it is the oldest remaining wrought iron truss bridge in the Cuyahoga Valley. Engineers developed metal bridges during the mid-1800s to respond to the growing railroad traffic and the need for a more durable material. As bridge construction transitioned from wood to metal, iron was briefly used before it was quickly replaced by the superior qualities of steel.

The bridge has been disassembled, taken to Elmira, New York, to be refurbished, brought back, and reassembled. Crossing the old iron bridge, we have a beautiful look at the high, multi-arching bridge of State Route 82, reflected in the waters of the Cuyahoga River.

The trail continues north on the Ohio and Erie Canal Towpath through the Cuyahoga Valley National Park. We pass a feeder canal where the system still operates, but the structure has been upgraded from stone block to concrete.

Cleveland Metropark Path

Shortly, we see another information display about a mud catcher dam, located across the canal on a tributary. Normally, an aqueduct is built to carry a canal over tributaries, but this tributary was allowed to flow into the canal. To hold back sediment that could fill a canal section, a concrete structure was built as a miniature dam. The sediment would settle behind the dam and then be cleaned out during a dry period. It's obvious, though, that the dam is not currently being maintained, because sediment has filled in behind it and is now also filling the canal. We see a few ducks and catch our first good look at a muskrat swimming in the canal.

The Buckeye Trail heads up the Sagamore Creek valley. Surprisingly, there is a good-sized, horseshoe-shaped waterfall. It's hard to estimate its height as we look down onto the falls from our ledge above. The falls is only a trickle today, but during a heavy rainfall it must look quite spectacular. A sign later informs us this is Linda Falls. We pass several other ledges and cascades as the trail continues up Sagamore Creek.

Reaching a paved bike trail, we pass a couple groups of deer. They must be "park deer"—protected from hunters and showing no fear of humans. The deer, perhaps 70 feet away, stand and stare at us. They are much smaller than the deer we saw in southern Ohio.

Cuyahoga Valley National Park Towpath Bike Trail

FAMILY AND HOME

Cicadas, we have been told, had a particularly large outbreak in this area of Ohio, evidenced by the dead tree twigs we've been seeing. Cicadas lay their eggs on the small ends of tree branches, splitting the bark and depositing the eggs. This weakens the branch, and the twig tip dies. A female may lay 400 to 600 eggs. When the eggs hatch, wingless cicada nymphs fall to the ground, and the dead twigs, which we are seeing now, fall off on their own. The nymphs burrow into the soil and feed on tree root sap until they emerge years later.

About four miles after Linda Falls, we pass the beautiful Bridal Veil Falls. Water is flowing in the stream, but it is not the best time for waterfalls. After a rain, the falls would be much more spectacular.

The entire day has been pleasant hiking. For the most part, our walk was on good trails through woods, past a canal, over an iron bridge, and past waterfalls. The trail was busy; many people are out walking or bicycling. It's a holiday weekend, but I imagine that these trails are normally more heavily used on weekends, since they are so near major metropolitan areas.

One lady bicyclist stops to ask, "Are you training for a big hike?" We explain what we are doing, and she seems impressed—she had no idea of the extent of the Buckeye Trail. Her interest also stems from the fact that she knows a person who hiked the Appalachian Trail and who has done some other long hikes as well.

The Hampton Inn is 0.7 mile off the trail. At the hotel, we shower and I work out our new hiking plan, since we had to alter today's hike.

It is 7 p.m. before we pick up a quick carry-out of burritos, mashed potatoes, and biscuits at the Taco Bell/KFC across the street.

Day 74: July 4, Monday

We are up at 5 a.m., pack, and go to the hotel lobby for a very good continental breakfast. Hampton Inn is a bit more upscale and has many breakfast selections for a hungry hiker, including waffles, eggs, sausages, oatmeal, cold cereal, hard-boiled eggs, bagels, English muffins, raisin bread, and many different Danishes.

Back on the trail, we have a carbon copy of yesterday morning. It is cool, in the mid-50s, with an overcast sky. The bridle trail along the Bedford Chagrin Parkway is as wide as a road and easy to hike. Where the bridle trail crosses Fairfield Oval Road, a park deer stands staring at us. It slowly moves off along the road as we continue down the trail. The deer is probably annoyed that we were using its path.

It is the Fourth of July, and as we hike along, we reminisce about our past Fourths together. Last year (2015), we were at our home, enjoying the boat parade around the lake and neighborhood fireworks. In 2014, we were in Colorado, hiking the Colorado Trail. We had begun the 500-mile trail on July 1st and finished it 30 days later. That trail was surprisingly different than the High Sierra. In the High Sierra, tree line is around 10,000 feet; but in the Colorado Rockies, tree line is closer to 12,500 feet, and the trail is therefore through more woods and mountain views are restricted to breaks in the forest. In 2013, our first Fourth of July together, we were still meeting family members, making plans for a trip to hike the John Muir Trail, and watching the boat parade on the lake before retiring for the night about the time some neighbor began setting off fireworks.

As we approach our destination for today, Chagrin Falls, Beth spots a car pulling out of a parking lot, and not only do I see her run (a rare sight), but she is running with her backpack on. She catches up with the car and asks the lady for a ride into town.

During our two-mile ride, we learn that the woman's teenage daughter is currently on a backpacking trip. This could be the reason that she was so inclined to help us! Whatever the reason, we are happy for a ride into town. At the inn where we've made a reservation, we find that our room, "The Mill," is not ready; but we are permitted to leave our packs, and we take an unencumbered walk into the quaint little town.

The main attraction for us is the falls. The town built decks and steps down the riverbank for people to sit, enjoy the view, and have safe access to the river bed for pictures and playing near the water.

Imaginative Blaze

Chagrin Falls

At the top of the stairs is a historical plaque that reads as follows:

> The Chagrin River was named for Francois Sequin, a Frenchman who traded with Native Americans in Northeast Ohio circa 1742. The "High Falls" of the Chagrin River primarily attracted settlers from New England (circa 1833) seeking a location with ample water power. By the mid-nineteenth century an axe factory, a foundry, 2 flour mills, 4 woolen mills, 2 sawmills, 3 paper mills, and a woodenware factory had been built along the riverbanks in Chagrin Falls. The "High Falls" provided a power source for a gristmill, built in 1836 at this location. Today, only one factory remains in operation in the Village of Chagrin Falls.

Curious, we later ask our innkeeper about the last remaining factory. The last to close was a paper factory, and, from her recollection, it closed 10 years ago. Thus there are no original factories left in Chagrin Falls.

The town has the air of a street festival, with an antique car show along one of the streets, a city park running up the east side of the river, and many small shops for people inclined to browse.

Yours Truly restaurant is recommended for dinner and seems to be popular. It has a good menu selection, and the entrees that people are eating look delicious. Beth and I both order the chopped salad with salmon and a side of their soft, coin-size potato chips. In the back of the restaurant is a patio garden sitting area. We place our order as a carry-out and head to a patio table to eat.

We are back in our room by 6:30 p.m.

It is raining, and the radar shows that the 15 percent chance of rain may be around for the next hour. I work on notes and Beth, who is tired, waits impatiently for hiker midnight.

Day 75: July 5, Tuesday

This morning begins with a delicious breakfast, continental-style but with many excellent choices.

A cab takes us back to the trail. The calm air is thick with a mist from last evening's rain, and when the trail passes through the woods, moisture drips from the leaves. The temperature is about 15 degrees warmer than yesterday morning, and that combined with the humidity quickly makes us perspire.

Everything north of the polo fields along Chagrin River Road speaks of wealth. Farms have beautiful fences and grazing horses. The small community of Gates Mills is a picturesque little town with all houses, large and small, immaculately landscaped. A footbridge in the town takes us across the Chagrin River.

We cross the Chagrin River three times today. At each crossing, the bridge is a different design and the river has a slightly different character to it.

Entering Chapin Forest Park, the trail passes a picnic shelter where two ladies, perhaps in their early 70s, are sitting at a table. They become curious as we approach. When we mention we are hiking the Buckeye Trail, they perk up and proudly tell us they have hiked, in sections, the entire northeast loop, which is a couple hundred miles. They're fascinated by our thru-hike; at one point, they had wanted to section hike the entire trail, but now they feel they're too old to begin such a long process.

On the west end of the park, the Quarry Pond shelter is near a quarry that supplied sandstone for the community of Kirtland during the 1800s. The quarried sandstone was used in the construction of the Mormon Kirtland Temple as well as other local homes and buildings. Mormon workers spent long days cutting stone, drying it in the sun, then driving stone-loaded wagons to the temple site two miles north. Joseph Smith, founder and first church president, served as quarry foreman. The temple was begun in 1833 and completed in 1836.

Wide Trail in the Metropark

At State Route 306, we call a cab to take us to the Days Inn motel, and we let him know we would appreciate a 6 a.m. pickup tomorrow to return us to the trail.

Tonight is our last night on the Buckeye Trail. Again, we look back at the ending of our John Muir Trail hike. On the last night, we were at Guitar Lake, at the base of the tallest mountain in the lower 48 states, Mount Whitney. From our tent flap, we could look out at the massive mountain yet to be climbed. We could not see a trail leading up the mountain, but according to the map, we would head up a valley before zigzagging up the mountain to the trail that traverses across to the mountain peak. The setting sun lit the mountain in a golden glow. Gradually, long shadows crept up the mountainside until the last golden rays on the peak blinked out.

We looked forward to our final day on the JMT and climbing that mountain. During the hike, we had shared spectacular views, made difficult climbs over passes, watched glorious morning sunrises, seen mountains reflected in still lakes, met fellow hikers, endured storms, and shared the close confines of a two-person tent. The journey had been challenging and rewarding. I had learned I was with a companion I could count on for comfort and support in the face of adversity.

As we circled Ohio, we have again tested our belief in each other. The challenges were greater and the time commitment longer. But the bonds that hold us together withstood the test. We have each other, and may we always be able to look into the eyes of the other and know that we will find support and unconditional love. We have so many more memories of what Ohio has to offer.

There are memories waiting, too, for those willing to venture onto a trail that is still young and undiscovered by the masses. The trail is what you make it. There are rock ledges, waterfalls, lazy rivers, rushing streams, lakes, state parks, conservancy districts, Native American ceremonial mounds, covered bridges, canal towpaths, boat rides, pioneer homesteads, military campaigns, and museums of bicycles, airplanes, presidents, and early Ohio military forts. Add to that, people to meet, with stories of their own to share. All this is calling to anyone willing to listen to the footsteps of people who have walked before them.

Day 76: July 6, Wednesday

Our final day begins at 5 a.m. After a quick (and last) motel continental breakfast, the cab takes us back to the trail.

It is a calm and warm 70-degree morning. Much of the morning walk is on sidewalk or a bikeway that parallels the neighborhood roads. Along the way, we find a nickel and quarter, to bring our BT total find to $3.05. Our completion celebration will really be fun!

About six miles before our goal, we enter the Mentor Marsh Nature Preserve. At the trailhead, a plaque gives us this information:

> For 200 years, the Mentor Lagoons have had a major impact on northeastern Ohio and its people. Located on the site of a large estuary where the Grand River once flowed into Lake Erie, the area evolved into a large marsh. It was here in 1797 that Charles Parker, a member of Moses Cleaveland's survey party, platted lands for the Connecticut Land Company and established the "Marsh Settlement," the first in what later became Lake County. Throughout the twentieth century, attempts were made to commercially develop this natural treasure, the most recent occurring in 1996. The proposed destruction of the Mentor Lagoons' pristine lakefront, upland forest and riverine marsh prompted Mentor voters to call for its preservation. For the first time in Ohio's history, voters affirmed eminent domain action to protect open space. This led to the city's acquisition of the 450-acre tract, now known as the Mentor Lagoons Nature Preserve and Marina.

A mile into the preserve, the trail passes along a small bluff overlooking Lake Erie. It is our first view of the lake since our start date of April 22. We are glad we used Lake Erie as our starting point. Such a vast body of water is a dramatic sight, and the impact of that view is heightened because it means that our trip is nearly complete.

FAMILY AND HOME

The trail goes through a small subdivision before again entering a wooded stretch for two of the last three miles.

The last half-mile is on a walkway parallel to the lake in Headlands Beach State Park. We are so close to completing this circle around Ohio, and we have been through so much together on this hike—tough times and exciting times. This last stretch is an emotional walk for us both.

The excitement rises as we look down the walkway and see family and friends waiting to celebrate with us. They are cheering and taking pictures as we meet them, and then, at the northern terminus of the Buckeye Trail, we're sharing handshakes, hugs, and words of congratulations.

Those who came to congratulate us are Beth's parents, Dave and Ruth, her brother, Michael, my sister Sue and her husband, Brad, and two members of the BTA, Jim Sprague and Bob Morecki.

Welcome at the Northern Terminus

Sue and Brad have made a two-by-three-foot congratulatory poster showing the Buckeye Trail, the dates of our hike, and a list of other hikes Beth and I have completed. Sue's artistic talent has done it beautifully. She even threw in two balloons to add to the festive air.

Celebrating Ohio with Buckeye Cookies!

FAMILY AND HOME

We do not have to dip into our "money findings" to make the occasion. Sue and Brad have provided croissants, tuna fish salad, tea, Gatorade, chips and salsa, and Bing cherries—enough for everyone. As an appropriate dessert, Sue made "Buckeye" cookies that are a hit with everyone. We take some of the cookies home as a continuing reminder of our celebration.

We chat about the trail and how friends and family are doing, and all too soon, we need to part company and head to the place we call home.

⊕ ⊕

Our last day on the John Muir Trail also saw us up early, breaking camp in the darkness. In the distance, we could see the glow of headlamps outlining the switchbacks that snake up out of the valley. Other hikers were already on the trail to Mt. Whitney.

After hiking up the mountain, we reached the pass where a hiker must choose to continue over to the town of Lone Pine or take the 1.9-mile side trail to the summit. The side trail is not steep; it follows a ridge to the summit. A hiker must also return on the same trail, so a row of backpacks had assembled at the junction. Beth and I also left ours there; we were wearing every piece of clothing we had, layering against the near-freezing temperature and blowing wind.

I took something else from my backpack to carry with me—a special quartzite stone.

We reached the summit, a broad and relatively flat jumble of mammoth flat boulders. One point is considered the highest on the mountain and is marked by a plaque. We took some time to look around.

Then I pulled out that special stone, got down on one knee, and asked Beth to marry me.

My words were barely out before she was pulling me up in a hug, saying, *Yes! Yes!*

Later, Beth did receive a diamond ring. And what became of the quartz stone? It was creatively wrapped with a strand of gold wire by her niece, Ruth Ann, who made it into a necklace. The gold strand looks like veins of gold in the quartz.

Our finish to the Buckeye Trail has not been quite so emotional, but Beth and I now have a home to return to together. Family members supported us in this adventure; trail angels helped us in times of need; friendly people gave us well wishes, smiles, and waves. We have seen much of Ohio, in a way that few will experience it.

Our memories are threaded together by a wandering path called the Buckeye Trail.

Thru-hike completed at northern terminus

Following page: Finish at Lake Erie

WANDERING OHIO

APPENDIX

APPENDIX

75 nights on the BT

*campsite w/shower
** campsite, no shower & possibly no water

1. **Stealth camp along bikeway near Chardon (water in town)
2. Red Maple Inn, Burton
3. **Camp Asbury (water from house before the camp)
4. Rocking Horse B&B, Ravenna
5. Joanne and Denny's home (pickup at Mogadore)
6. **Quail Hollow Park Campground (water in towns)
7. **Nimisila Campground (water in towns)
8. **Pittman Park, Navarre (water in towns)
9. **Camp Tuscazoar (water in towns)
10. Sue & Brad's Farm Cabin (pickup at Leesville Marina)
11. *Tappan Lake Campground
12. *Piedmont Campground
13. Salt Fork State Park Lodge
14. Salt Fork State Park Lodge
15. *Seneca Lake Parkside Campground
16. *Wolf Run State Park Campground
17. **Road Fork Lean-to
18. **Lamping Homestead
19. **Campsite near Great Cave
20. **Self-made "Rough" campsite along trail
21. **Wrangler Restaurant property, Whipple (water at restaurant)
22. **Farmhouse front lawn (water at house)
23. Stockport Mill Inn
24. Stockport Mill Inn
25. **Russ Tippett's lawn (water at house)
26. Burr Oak Lodge
27. **Murray City ballfield
28. **Old Stone Church Trailhead campsite
29. Bear Run B&B
30. Baymont Inn, Logan
31. Hocking Hills Park Cabin (w/Sue & Brad)
32. Hocking Hills Park Cabin (w/Sue & Brad)
33. **Mr. Detty's property
34. **Scioto Trail State Park Campground (water, but no shower)
35. *Mapleberry Farm
36. *Pike Lake State Park Campground
37. *Butler Springs Christian Camp

WANDERING OHIO

38. **Serpent Mound Shelter (water at museum)
39. *Mineral Springs Lake Resort Campground
40. Ben's Happy Trail Horse Camp
41. Shawnee State Park Lodge
42. Shawnee State Park Lodge
43. **Don Fiedler's "hunters" cabin (water at house)
44. Country Inn, West Union
45. Bailey House, Georgetown
46. Bailey House, Georgetown
47. Laura's home (Beth's cousin), Cincinnati
48. Laura's home (Beth's cousin), Cincinnati
49. *Little Miami Canoe Livery Campsite, Morrow
50. Lori's Home, Spring Valley
51. Mark Heise's home, Yellow Springs
52. Hotel Dayton
53. Days Inn, Tipp City
54. Arrowston B&B, Piqua
55. Arrowston B&B, Piqua
56. **Boy Scout Shelter
57. *Fort Loramie State Park campground
58. America's Best Value Inn, St Marys
59. Red Carpet Motel, Delphos
60. Nothing but Nature cabin
61. Super 8 motel, Defiance
62. Best Western, Napoleon
63. Mill House B&B
64. Days Inn, Bowling Green
65. Days Inn, Fremont
66. Days Inn, Fremont
67. Victorian Tudor Inn B&B, Bellevue
68. Victoria Lady B&B, Norwalk
69. *Findley Lake State Park Campground
70. Red Roof Inn, Medina
71. Red Roof Inn, Medina
72. Michael's House (Beth's brother), Stow
73. Hampton Inn, Solon
74. Chagrin Falls Inn
75. Days Inn, Willoughby

31 nights of tent camping
44 nights at hotel, park lodge, cabin, or B&B

APPENDIX

Camping Gear Weight (Chuck)

lbs	oz	
1	14.0	Backpack: Gossamer Mariposa (Large: ~4200 cu in)
	4.1	Pack cover
1	9.0	Z-Tent (2-person)
	3.7	Stakes (8)
	7.8	Tyvek ground cloth
1	1.2	Therm-a-Rest
2	0.0	Sleeping bag (down 20F)
	4.4	Silk liner
	1.7	Food bag - grey
	5.0	"Kitchen sink" container
1	2.0	Water filter
	2.8	Water purifier (Na hypochlorite)
	4.3	Water bag (3 Liter)
3	12.5	Personal Items [see following list]
	4.4	Flip flops
1	0.6	PrimaLoft coat
	11.2	Rain jacket
	8.9	Rain pants
	7.9	Swing Trek Umbrella
	1.4	LL Bean Fleece Hat
	2.3	OR VersaLiner Glove
	0.8	VersaLiner shells
	6.0	Underwear x 3 (2 oz each)
	4.0	Socks x 2 (2 oz/pair)
	1.8	CoolMax Wright socks
	5.6	T-shirt
	8.4	T-shirt
	11.0	Long sleeve
	4.7	Swimsuit
	5.0	Journal
1	0.4	Trail data & Google town maps
1	2.0	Trail maps
	3.0	Gatorade 20oz bottles (2) (1.5 oz. ea)
		Food (2.5 lbs/day)

22.1 lbs Total (plus food & water)

Wear	oz	
	13.6	REI Zip-off pants (beige)
	6.3	T-shirt
2	14	Trail shoes (Altra - Lone Peak)
1	5	Poles
	2.9	REI smart wool sock
	2	Underwear
	0.5	Sunglasses
	6.2	Camera
	1	Hat light

Personal Items
ounces

1	Vicks
5.1	Hydrogen peroxide
1.5	Tinactin
1	Swim-EAR
1.4	Bug repellent
0.2	Water tablets
3.2	Medications (pills)
5.1	Phone
2.6	Phone cord
2.4	Shaver cord
2.3	Camera batt charger
1.2	Camera battery (0.6 x2)
6.4	Phone 3x battery
0.6	Thermometer/clip
1.2	Washcloth
1.8	Pack towel
0.4	Toothbrush
1.0	Toothpaste
3.0	Shampoo
1.0	Nail clipper & file
6.4	Electric shaver
0.2	Comb
1.0	Toilet paper
2.4	Head light (WalMart)
0.4	Sharpie
7.7	Misc (zip locks, etc)
60.5	**Total (ounces) [i.e. 3 lbs 12.5 oz]**

APPENDIX

Camping Gear Weight (Beth)

lbs	oz	
1	12.0	Backpack: Gossamer Gorilla (Small: 2300 cu in)
	3.4	Pack cover
1	3.5	Therm-a-Rest
2	5.0	Sleeping bag
	4.0	Silk liner
1	4.6	Personal Items (see list on next page)
	5.9	flip flops
1	1.0	PrimaLoft coat
	9.2	Rain jacket
	11.0	Rain pants
	7.9	Swing Trek Umbrella
	3.3	Poncho
	0.8	Thermasilk liner gloves
	1.7	OR VersaLiner Glove
	0.6	VersaLiner shells
	2.6	Underwear x 3 (1 oz each) & Long(3.6)
	1.0	Silk liner socks (1.0) x1
	5.5	Wright socks (1.2) x3
	7.3	NYC Shirt
	4.0	T-shirt
	5.4	Shorts –extra (Dri-Star)
	1.0	Glasses
	1.2	Baggies
	3.0	Gatorade 20oz bottles (2) (1.5 oz. each)

12.6 lbs Total (plus food & water)

Wear	oz.	
	11.6	REI Zip-off pants (black)
	6.0	T-shirt
1	1.6	Altra – Lone Peak Trail Shoes
1	1.0	Poles
	1.8	Llama sock
	0.7	Underwear
	2.6	Ball cap
	1.2	Sunglasses

Personal Items
ounces

0.2	Camphor
0.2	Ear plugs
1.0	Lozenges
0.6	Repair kit
1.9	Bug repellent
0.8	Washcloth
1.6	Pack towel
1.4	Body lotion
1.2	Face wash
0.5	Face cream
0.3	Toothbrush
1.0	Toothpaste
1.2	Rescue remedy
0.2	Honey cream
2.0	Sunscreen
0.2	Lip gloss
0.8	Deodorant
1.5	Toilet paper
0.3	Comb
0.4	Flashlight
0.8	Mole skin/bandaids
2.5	Laundry detergent

Total = 20.6   [i.e. 1 lb   4.6 oz]

Made in the USA
Lexington, KY
29 September 2019